Reinventing the Future

GLOBAL GOALS FOR THE 21st CENTURY

Reinventing the Future

GLOBAL GOALS FOR THE 21st CENTURY

Rushworth M. Kidder
Senior Columnist,
The Christian Science Monitor

The MIT Press
Cambridge, Massachusetts
London, England

This book was set in Garamond by The Christian Science Publishing Society.
Book design by Kenneth J. Wilson (Wilson Graphics & Design).
Jacket design and illustration by Genegraphics, Boston.
Printed and bound in the U.S.A. by Semline Book Group.

Library of Congress Cataloging-in-Publication Data

Reinventing the Future: Global Goals for the 21st Century.

Includes Index.
1. Twenty-first century—Forecasts.   I. Kidder, Rushworth M.
Library of Congress Catalog Card Number: 89-061951

ISBN 0-262-11146-2

Contents

Preface———————————————————————

As this book goes to press, the year 2000 is little more than a decade away.

If recent history is a reliable guide, the turn of the century —of the millennium, in fact—will galvanize attention around the world. The celebrations surrounding the American Bicentennial, in 1976, the commemoration of the signing of the Constitution of the United States, in 1987, the forthcoming five-hundredth anniversary of Columbus's discovery of the New World in 1992: these will pale before the blaze attending the year 2000. It will roar in aboard a worldwide New Year's bash of parades, fireworks, television extravaganzas, and yet-to-be-invented forms of hype, hoopla, and ballyhoo. And, since the 21st century doesn't officially begin until January 1, 2001, it will have a full year to play itself out.

But what will be the real significance of the arrival of the new millennium? How will we celebrate it in thought as well as action? What key ideas will we take with us into the future?

If humanity, accustomed to making resolutions on New Year's Eve, turns its attention to New Century's resolutions, what will it have to say? What will be the major, first-intensity issues facing the world as the new century opens? If we are serious about addressing them, how far can we reasonably expect to move along the path toward solutions during the next 129 months?

Those questions and others arose during conversations I had in early 1987 with Michael K. Hooker, the youthful and energetic President of the University of Maryland at Baltimore County. He was one of a number of people I had interviewed for a series in *The Christian Science Monitor,* which was later published as *An Agenda for the 21st Century* (Cambridge, Mass.: MIT Press, 1987). As we finished, Hooker opened up a whole new range of thinking with a simple question: What next?

His answer was disarmingly concrete. He proposed that we gather together as many of the interviewees as possible around a quiet conference table somewhere, add a number of other thoughtful people, and refine our vision of the future. As we talked further, the nature of that refinement became clearer. The *Monitor* series and book had already identified a six-point agenda of major issues facing the next century: nuclear warfare, the population crisis, environmental degradation, the North-South gap between the developed and the developing world, the worldwide need for education reform, and the breakdown of public and private morality. Was it not the logical next step, then, to set some goals for addressing those concerns that would be reasonable, practical, and reachable? What should those goals be? By the year 2000, how far could we reasonably expect to have come in addressing the 21st century's most pressing concerns?

Like so many good ideas, this one might still be sleeping peacefully in its folder had it not been for the enthusiasm of William B. Boyd. As president (now retired) of the Johnson Foundation, Bill oversaw the operations of one of the nation's most remarkable conference facilities: Wingspread, a home designed by Frank Lloyd Wright in Racine, Wisconsin, for the family that founded the Johnson Wax Company. Inviting us to use his facility, he also added a simple idea that proved vital to our progress. He persuaded us to invite members of what he calls "the successor generation" of younger thinkers who will be coming into their own in the 21st century.

And so it was that, from April 14 through 16, 1987, thirty-five individuals from twelve nations gathered at Wingspread for a conference entitled "Agenda 2000: Reasonable Goals." The charge to this group was global in scope. They were to identify a set of reasonable goals for humanity. The goals were to be attainable by the year 2000—neither so vast as to be unrealistic, nor so easily reached as to be insignificant. Finally, they were to focus on the next century's most pressing problems.

A word about the topics chosen for discussion is in order. We had originally planned three sessions: on East-West relations, on North-South relations (including population), and on environmental concerns (including quality-of-life and ethical issues). So keen were the participants to consider ethics on its own, however, that we adjusted the schedule to make room for a full discussion of that topic—surely a telling sign of the importance that should attach to ethical matters in any consideration of global futures.

Unlike some conferences, ours kept formal presentations to a minimum. There were no real lectures, no readings of papers, no panel discussions. Only at the end, when we set about drafting the statements of goals, did we break for an hour into small groups. We were, instead, a committee of the whole, pursuing our topics around a room full of statement and dialogue, point and counterpoint, raised hands and polite interruptions. Not surprisingly, the conference produced some of the most stimulating conversation I've participated in during my ten years with *The Christian Science Monitor.*

Drawing on a transcript of our meetings, I assembled a twelve-page report that appeared in the *Monitor* several months later. This book is an attempt to capture even more fully the ethos of those three days. No mere transcript, it is instead a journey among ideas, an attempt to weave together into a coherent whole the underlying substance of our discussions. I have adhered rigorously to the actual language used by each speaker. I have engaged in (and often agonized over) the lightest editing only where I felt that a point needed clarifying and that the intrusion of ellipses or brackets would needlessly clutter the page. I have, however, exercised more liberty in drawing together passages from different parts of our discussion—sometimes from different days—under single headings. That, I suppose, reflects the technique of the journalist, who builds an article from numerous interviews at different times and places, respecting the context of each comment but feeling no need to present quotations in the order in which he or she first heard them.

I've also tried to let the voices speak for themselves—even when, on a few occasions, I found myself less than fully in agreement with them. And, knowing the historian's requirement for keeping the reader engaged and rewarded, I've been guided by something written years ago by the late Barbara Tuchman—who had agreed to join us at Wingspread but canceled most reluctantly under the pressure of a manuscript deadline. "Above all," she says in her book *Praticing History,* "discard the irrelevant."

Not to be discarded, however, are the tremendous thanks owed to all those who made the conference and the book possible. The three institutions cosponsoring the conference—*The Christian Science Monitor,* the Johnson Foundation, and the University of Maryland at Baltimore County—deserve first mention. Adam Yarmolinsky, Provost of the latter and more than simply our moderator, was a stalwart in helping plan the event and invite the participants. Rita Goodman, vice president (now retired) of the Johnson Foundation, poured herself into the details with a diligence and thoughtfulness that combined the best elements of motherhood with the highest sense of professionalism. Each of the thirty-five participants gave much more than can possibly be reflected here: The transcript, registering only their public and plenary comments, missed the hundreds of hallway, dinner-table, and late-night conversations among small groups that, I'm told, continue to this day.

Sherry L. Schiller, president of Countdown 2001 in Washington, D.C., provided invaluable counsel and encouragement along the way. Great thanks are due to all those at the *Monitor* who saw and supported the promise of both the conference and the book: John Hoagland, Richard Ralston, Katherine Fanning, David Anable, David Winder, and David Holmstrom. This book, in particular, owes much to those who labored over its editing and production, including David Hohle, Thomas D'Evelyn, and Carolyn Marsh. Finally, it never would have come about had not my wife and daughters sustained and supported its composition. To them I owe the benefits of a warm and friendly family life—which, of all the reasonable goals the 21st century could strive for, is surely one of the most valuable.

Camden, Maine
February 1989

Chapter 1

"The Courage to Be an Amateur"

Andrei Voznesensky is a study in contrasts. One of the Soviet Union's best-known poets, he has a keen interest in global affairs. A reticent man, he will suddenly open up and talk for minutes on end with a passion born of deep thought. A natty dresser — hardly the image of a scruffy modern poet — he declaims his poems in a voice that alternately whispers and roars, and with an abandon that raises gooseflesh or shakes rafters. A world traveler who could have defected any number of times, he so loves his homeland that he's recently been known to turn down invitations from abroad in order to stay close to the buddings of *glasnost* at Moscow rock concerts or gallery openings.

At the beginning of that weekend in Wisconsin, however, he was playing the listener's role. Like the other thirty-four people from twelve nations assembled in the high-ceilinged, wood-paneled meeting room overlooking a meandering stream, he had come to Wingspread to help forge a set of global goals for the year 2000. And like the rest of us, he had been captivated by the ambience.

That's understandable. Wingspread is the largest of the many single-family homes designed by Frank Lloyd Wright. Sitting on forty acres of gently rolling fields and woods along the Lake Michigan shore in Racine, Wisconsin, it was built for Herbert F. Johnson of the Johnson Wax Company. The sprawling, earth-toned house is now a conference center run by the Johnson Foundation. In keeping with the corporate interests of its founder, it's a showcase of housekeeping—so well polished, in fact, that a television crew filming some of our participants found that when they tried to use their silver gaffer's tape to hold cords against the hardwood paneling, it wouldn't stick.

For Andrei Voznesensky, however, Wingspread was more symbol than showcase. Trained as an architect, he recognized Wright's building from pictures he had seen at the Architectural Institute in Moscow in the 1950s. Nor did the irony of its symbolism escape him. It was built, he reminded us, by an architect who was already a "man of the 21st century." The year was 1937, the time of Stalin's greatest crimes.

So on that April Friday, as our group turned its attention to East-West relations, that symbolism was part of the moment. Gail Lapidus, chair of the Berkeley-Stanford Program on Soviet International Behavior and a professor at the University of California-Berkeley, set the stage. Her discussion of Soviet leader Mikhail Gorbachev's reforms and their effect on the future of East-West relations was in the best tradition of American political science.[1]

She spoke eloquently about the opportunities and dangers of *perestroika*—the attempt to restructure a society where generations of military domination, stolid bureaucracy, and inward-looking isolationism stand entrenched against the waves of global communication, commercial enterprise, and democratic ideals now breaking across Soviet borders. The conversation that followed zeroed in on tough but attainable goals for East-West relations at the turn of the century.

And still Voznesensky sat quietly. His chin propped on his hands, he followed the conversation with his eyes. Finally Adam Yarmolinsky, our moderator, turned to him for his comments. He paused a moment, not with any sense of criticism, but as though to summon inspiration. When he at last spoke, in a rough-cut English empowered by something other than grammar, his words put us into an entirely new register of thought.

"You see," he began softly, "the problem we are talking about now, for me it is not only theoretical problem. For me it is life and death, and life or death not only for my country but me personally. Is not so easy.

"You can see Mr. Gorbachev, smiling and charming person, on TV. But he's very rigid person, because for the first time in our history he tries to change country, to modernize country, by democratic way. But here we in our country have eighteen millions of *nomenclatura* bureaucracy who are against Gorbachev—eighteen millions, not eighteen thousands, who are against him!

"You spoke now," he continued, gesturing to Yarmolinsky, "and asked what guarantee, what hope [that democracy would succeed]. I don't know what will be. It is fight. Maybe it will not be victory. I have no guarantee because I have to be sincere to you. Democracy is terrible thing in our country. We had no democracy for 1000 years. It is impossible to have a good economy now without democracy; and it is first time when so-called revolution is coming by intellectuals with ideas, by media, by publishing books, by poetry readings.

"I am not from government, I am not member of Communist party, but, if you help this process [in] connection with Gorbachev, you help democracy in the whole world.

"I want you to help us to come into the 21st century," he added. "Really, we need your help."

There was more, much more, that he said. But in the silence that followed as he sat back in his chair, it was Amitai Etzioni who raised his hand and caught the moderator's eye.

In a way, here too was a study in contrasts. Prof. Etzioni, a German-born American sociologist now teaching at Harvard

3

and author of ten books, has been called, only half-facetiously, "the everything expert." Avoiding the narrow specializations that academic research sometimes demands, he is a committed generalist who, like a poet, sees everything in life as grist for the mill. Like Voznesensky, he too has known something of hardship, having fled with his parents from anti-Semitic Nazi Germany to Palestine in 1936, and later having joined the Jewish underground in the war for Israeli independence from the British. So when he spoke directly to the poet in his own still-strong accent, his words came from the heart and spoke for us all.

"I think this calls for at least, if not an excellent round of applause, an expression of our delight," he said. "Those of us who have attended meetings over the last twenty years with members of your country and had to put up with party cant are absolutely celebrating and delighting that we can hear you say what you're saying.

"If there is a future, and if there is a change, if the Soviet Union allows more people like you to come to the forefront, I think it calls for some recognition."

When he finished amid murmers of assent from around the table, Yarmolinksy noted that "we will record a round of applause." And that's what the conference transcript shows.

In the months since our meeting, I've often recalled this interchange. It wasn't simply that East met West. That happens, fortunately, quite often these days. Nor was it that the words themselves, even when taken out of context and held up to scrutiny, were particularly notable. It was that the moment distilled the spirit of the Wingspread conference. It spoke eloquently of the value of gathering individuals representing all walks of life in a variety of nations together in one room to ask one of the greatest of life's questions: Where do we go from here?

That's not a question for specialists: There are no professors of 21st century goals, no government agencies devoted to seeing life whole, no books that teach global eclecticism. Nor were those of us around the table specialists in the subject at hand. To be sure, the participants came out of various specialties. But they were acting as generalists. Voznesensky was not speaking as a poet when he called on the rest of us to help his nation come into the 21st century. And Etzioni was not speaking as a sociologist when he thanked him. They were speaking as humanitarians, fellow citizens of a world tumbling headlong into a new millennium.

What brought them together? The common conviction that something had to be done concerning the four broad issues on the conference agenda — East-West relations, the North-South gap between the developing and the industrial world, the degradation of the global environment, and the breakdown in public and private morality. To be sure, there were diplomats, economists, environmentalists, and philosophers at the table: specialists in our four agenda areas. But the agenda itself would not allow them to remain in their specialties. They had to participate in the entire discussion, not simply in its separate parts. For these three days, at least, theirs was the role of Sophocles who Matthew Arnold said "saw life steadily, and saw it whole."

But why this emphasis on wholeness? In part, the answer is a practical one. The world needs goals, and someone needs to set them. But who? Not, surely, the specialists arguing for particular sets of specialized solutions. They will tend, naturally and properly, to see their own particular area of interest as the foremost issue on the global agenda. Instead, the overview needs to be taken by generalists capable of comprehending diverse viewpoints and arguing for the broad range of ideas that, taken together, will most benefit humanity.

Put another way, the need is for a broader recognition of

one of the outstanding facts of modern life: global interdependence. As the world becomes increasingly interlinked, there are two key arguments for the generalist's approach. The first touches on relationships among problems once thought to be discrete. A decade ago, this factor figured strongly in the Brandt Report, prepared in 1980 by the Independent Commission on International Development Issues under the chairmanship of former West German Chancellor Willy Brandt. In his introduction, Brandt put it this way:

> We are increasingly confronted with more and more problems which affect mankind as a whole, so that solutions to these problems are inevitably internationalized. The globalization of dangers and challenges—war, chaos, self-destruction—calls for a domestic policy which goes much beyond parochial or even national items. Yet this is happening at a snail's pace. A rather defensive pragmatism still prevails, when what we need are new perspectives and bold leadership for the real interests of people and mankind. The "international community" is still too cut off from the experience of ordinary people, and vice versa.

> Quite a number of problems are becoming common to societies with differing political regimes. They could be called system-bridging: ranging from energy to ecology, from arms limitation to redistribution of employment, from micro-electronics to new scientific options which today are only faintly outlined. Whether these matters are discussed in Boston or Moscow, in Rio or Bombay, everywhere there are people who see their whole planet involved, at a breathtaking pace, in the same problems of energy shortage, urbanization with environmental pollution, and highly sophisticated technology which threatens to ignore human values and which people may not be able to handle adequately.[2]

Brandt's point has recently been seconded in the Brundtland Report, presented to the United Nations General Assembly in 1987 by the World Commission on Environment and Development, chaired by Norwegian Prime Minister Gro

6

Brundtland. On the subject of "the interlocking crises," the report's authors write:

> Until recently, the planet was a large world in which human activities and their effects were neatly compartmentalized within nations, within sectors (energy, agriculture, trade), and within broad areas of concern (environmental, economic, social). These compartments have begun to dissolve. This applies in particular to the various global "crises" that have seized the public concern, particularly over the past decade. These are not separate crises: an environmental crisis, a development crisis, an energy crisis. They are all one.[3]

The second key argument flowing from global interdependence is the growing inability of present specializations to provide answers, a point also discussed in the Brundtland Report:

> When the century began, neither human numbers nor technology had the power radically to alter planetary systems. As the century closes, not only do vastly increased human numbers and their activities have that power, but major, unintended changes are occurring in the atmosphere, in soils, in waters, among plants and animals, and in the relationships among all of these. *The rate of change is outstripping the ability of scientific disciplines and our current capabilities to assess and advise.* It is frustrating the attempts of political and economic institutions, which evolved in a different, more fragmented world, to adapt and cope. It deeply worries many people who are seeking ways to place those concerns on the political agenda. (Italics added.)[4]

In a world where the "rate of change" demands "system-bridging" solutions, then, who can "assess and advise" on the world's most pressing problems? Where will the 21st century's solutions come from? The answer, it seems, lies in an originality of thinking that both builds upon and transcends today's specialties. But originality, by its very nature, breaks barriers and crosses boundaries, which is probably why the

American poet Wallace Stevens noted that "it is necessary to any originality to have the courage to be an amateur."

Who, then, were these original thinkers, these courageous amateurs, gathered at Wingspread? The list suggests their diversity:

JOAN ABRAHAMSON (U.S.), lawyer, painter, community activist, and MacArthur Fellow who founded the Jefferson Institute in Los Angeles, which seeks to develop creative solutions to public policy problems.

MEINHARD ADE (West Germany), director general of West German president Richard von Weizsacker's office.

NAZIR AHMAD (Bangladesh), graduate student in business at Stanford University and cofounder and director of the Overseas Development Network, which seeks to involve American students in international development issues.

JOHN ARAKA (Nigeria), chairman of the editorial board of the *Daily Times* in Lagos.

RODRIGO BOTERO (Colombia), former finance minister of Colombia, now at Harvard's Center for National Affairs, and a Ford Foundation trustee.

WILLIAM B. BOYD (U.S.), president (now retired) of the Johnson Foundation, president emeritus of the University of Oregon, and a cohost of the conference.

WILLIAM C. CLARK (U.S.), ecologist and policy analyst at Harvard's Kennedy School of Government and a MacArthur Fellow.

AMITAI ETZIONI (U.S.), visiting professor at the Harvard Business School, author of *Capital Corruption, An Immodest Agenda,* and, most recently, *The Moral Dimension: Towards a New Economics.*

DOUGLAS FRASER (U.S.), former president of the 1.1-million-member United Automobile Workers Union, currently a Professor of Labor Studies at Wayne State University.

THEODORE J. GORDON (U.S.), former chief engineer for the Saturn program at McDonnell-Douglas, founder of his own consulting firm, The Futures Group, in Glastonbury, Connecticut.

KRISTIN HELMORE (U.S.), free-lance writer; from 1984 to 1988, covered developing-world issues for *The Christian Science Monitor;* coauthor of a series on the global exploitation of children.

MICHAEL K. HOOKER (U.S.), president of the University of Maryland at Baltimore County, philosopher, student of contemporary culture, and a cohost of the conference.

MATINA HORNER (U.S.), president of Radcliffe College in Cambridge, Massachusetts.

EDWIN HUTCHINS (U.S.), cognitive and cultural anthropologist at the University of California-San Diego and a MacArthur Fellow.

SHUICHI KATO (Japan), social critic, poet, and author of a prize-winning history of Japanese literature, formerly professor of comparative literature at Sophia University in Tokyo.

RUSHWORTH M. KIDDER (U.S.), senior columnist for *The Christian Science Monitor,* author of *An Agenda for the 21st Century,* and a cohost of the conference.

RICHARD LAMM (U.S.), former governor of Colorado, author of *Megatraumas,* and recipient of the 1985 *Christian Science Monitor* Peace 2010 Essay Award.

GAIL W. LAPIDUS (U.S.), chair of the Berkeley-Stanford Program on Soviet International Behavior and a professor of political science at the University of California-Berkeley.

BRAD LEITHAUSER (U.S.), poet and fiction writer, professor of English at Amherst College, and MacArthur Fellow.

STELLA MARIA (Indonesia), director of the Women, Youth, and Child Institute at the All-Indonesian Workers Union in Jakarta.

ROBERT S. McNAMARA (U.S.), former president of the World Bank, former Secretary of Defense, and author of *Blundering into Disaster: Surviving the First Century of the Nuclear Age.*

PATRICK MUNGAI (Kenya), features editor of *The Daily Nation* in Nairobi.

VINEET NARAIN (India), staff reporter for the New Delhi newspaper *Jansatta,* the nation's leading Hindu newspaper, and a television-documentary broadcaster concentrating on rural development.

OLUSEGUN OBASANJO (Nigeria), former head of state of Nigeria and cochair of the Commonwealth Mission to South Africa (known as the Eminent Persons Group) in 1986.

TOMMY ODEMWINGIE (Nigeria), features editor of *The Guardian* in Lagos, and president of the Nigerian Club for Information on Children.

TINA ROSENBERG (U.S.), MacArthur Fellow and free-lance journalist living in Latin America.

KIM SHIPPEY (U.S.), senior anchor/producer for *The World Service of The Christian Science Monitor.*

KATHLEEN KENNEDY TOWNSEND (U.S.), director of the Maryland Student Service Alliance and cofounder of the Robert Kennedy Human Rights Award.

ANDREI VOZNESENSKY (USSR), Russian poet whose work has appeared in English translation (as *An Arrow in the Wall*) and in most Western European languages.

KATHARINE WHITEHORN (U.K.), columnist for the *Observer* in London.

SHIRLEY WILLIAMS (U.K.), former education minister, founder of the Social Democratic Party, and joint president of the newly constituted Social and Liberal Democrats.

GEORGE WOODWELL (U.S.), ecologist, founder and director of the Woods Hole Research Center, Cape Cod, Massachusetts.

ADAM YARMOLINSKY (U.S.), Provost of the University of Maryland at Baltimore County who served Presidents Kennedy, Johnson, and Carter at the Pentagon, the White House, and the Arms Control Agency.

BILLIE JEAN YOUNG (U.S.), MacArthur Fellow, poet, and performing artist working in Jackson, Mississippi, where she heads the Southern Women's Rural Network.

ZHANG YI (People's Republic of China), research associate from the Institute of American Studies in the Chinese Academy of Social Sciences in Peking.

A group of amateurs? In the business of global goals, yes: as is everyone. But not, clearly, in their accumulated years of insight and the breadth of their endeavors. They were invited for several reasons. Some had already appeared as

11

interviewees in the *Monitor*'s earlier series, "Agenda for the 21st Century." Some were chosen for their well-known contributions in areas relevant to the conference agenda. But quite a few came because, by the best standards we could find, they were destined to make future contributions. William Boyd, president of the Johnson Foundation, spoke of them as members of "the successor generation"—younger people who will play key roles in the twenty-first century and will, one way or another, have to live with the goals we established.

Again, however, it was Etzioni who put this group in its proper perspective. At the reception following our initial Thursday evening gathering, held in the pagoda-like living room under the ranks of clerestory windows, he gazed around at the voluble crowd. There was Vineet Narain in his Nehru jacket, Olusegun Obasanjo in his flowing robe and headdress, Billie Jean Young in her tight black braids. There was Tommy Odemwingie in his colorful African coat, Stella Maria in her embroidered jacket and flowing scarf, and Ed Hutchins in his open-necked white shirt. It was as though, Etzioni said, you took the globe and shook it, and then picked up an assortment of the people who fell off and put them all in one room.

None of that variety would have mattered, however, were it not for the work they accomplished during the next several days. By the beginning of our last session, according to my notes, we had identified ninety-five goals to be reached by the year 2000. The number, I'm sure, bears no real relationship to the ninety-five theses Martin Luther nailed to the door of the church at Wittenberg in 1517 to usher in the Reformation—especially since, in our final session, we reduced the list to a more workable number. Refining these goals, we drafted statements of the current problems and identified strategies for reaching the goals.

It is these, and the accounts of the discussions underlying

them, that occupy the following pages. None of which, I hasten to add, is meant to be definitive. The purpose of this conference and this book are the same: to stimulate further creativity and, no doubt, some controversy. Some of the points we discussed, like the proposal for a fuel tax, will spark opposition. Others may take years to refine, like the gathering of new sets of statistics on Third World nations. Still others seem both essential and inevitable, like the banning of chemical and biological weapons.

All, however, are offered with the intention of moving humanity forward. This book is not offered as yet another report, meant to sit quietly on a shelf and contribute footnotes to still more reports. If this book has one guiding purpose, it is to help generate the political will to address some of the major problems facing the world so that, when the fireworks and fanfare that will inevitably surround the great global birthday party for the year 2001 have died away, we will find ourselves further along toward reaching the goals that really matter.

Chapter 2

The North-South Gap

Global economic development simply isn't working.

That's a stark assessment. But Rodrigo Botero knows the subject too well to take a more rosy view. An economist and an engineer by training, and by disposition a thoughtful observer of the human scene in and around his native Colombia, he came of age in a period when it was fashionable to equate *development* with *money*. As his career matured through positions in academics, as head of his own private research institute, and as minister of finance under President Alfonso Lopez from 1974 to 1976, so did his views of development. Now, as a trustee of the Ford Foundation and past publisher of a Bogota-based periodical, *Estrategia,* devoted to economic and international affairs, he writes frequently on one of the most challenging of mankind's problems: the widening gulf between the wealthy, consumer-oriented industrial nations and the impoverished nations of the developing world.

So it was natural for us to ask him to introduce the issue of global development to our conference, to have him lay a foundation upon which a series of attainable goals could be constructed. We didn't realize quite how radical his suggestions would be.

"If I were to make one recommendation for the year 2000," Botero told our first working session, his voice quiet with conviction, "it would be simply to drop the goal of closing the gap, understood as it has been understood in the past thirty years."

That last phrase is crucial. Botero wants the gap closed. He's not arguing for the status quo. Nor is he calling for some sort of "zero-growth" option, which assumes that social progress can occur without economic development. Instead, he's seeking an entirely new method of measurement.

Why? The answer lies in decades of history. Traditionally, the gap between North and South, the developed and the developing world, has been measured by charting the flow and accumulation of money. The ranking of countries according to gross national product per capita (the total value of a nation's annual output of goods and services, divided by the size of its population) shows the breadth of the gap in no uncertain terms. According to World Bank figures for 1987, the United States has a per capita gross national product (GNP) of $18,430, Japan $15,770 and the United Kingdom $10,430. On the other side of the gap, Colombia has only $1,220. India, meanwhile, survives on $300, and Ethiopia on $120.

Down through the years, then, the temptation has been to equate well-being with per capita GNP, as though money, and money alone, measured the Western world's success. Such thinking was especially common, argues Botero, in the aftermath of World War II, when the fledgling field of development economics was coming into its own.

"When the international community got around to looking seriously at the relationships between developed and developing countries in the 1950s," he says, "the analogies that were utilized" were those of the Marshall Plan. The reconstruction of Europe and Japan, after all, had come about through huge infusions of capital. If such infusions could bring economic order out of postwar chaos, could not similar investments bring prosperity to a post-colonial Third World as well? So it was, he argues, that "well-intentioned, intelligent people looked at the developing world and said, 'If the conditions are set whereby they're supplied with the necessary capital, then the rest will follow.'"

For the leaders of developing nations, Botero notes, "this was music to their ears." They faced the daunting tasks of nation-building. How much easier, then, to follow a common path. The path would begin with capital from abroad, largely in the form of grants, loans, and manufacturing equipment. And it would end, or so it was thought, with industrial economies resembling those of the United States and Western Europe spread across the face of the planet.

By the 1960s, however, it was obvious that something was clearly amiss. The Pearson Commission—the Commission on International Development, convened by former Canadian Prime Minister Lester Pearson to examine the crisis in aid to developing-nation economies—found in 1969 that the gap, far from closing, was in fact increasing. Then came the 1973 oil shock and its quadrupling of petroleum prices. As the lingering twilight of a decades-long post-World War II economic expansion flickered out, whatever momentum the developing world had been riding ground to a halt.

And, of course, the North-South gap grew even wider. As it grew, so the consensus on global development shrank. Result: "The debate between the industrialized and the developing countries became much more acrimonious," notes Botero. It soon ceased, in fact, to be a "debate" at all. Instead, it became a pattern of "mutual accusations, a series of recriminations" turning on the question of who was to blame for the situation.

What had gone wrong? The expectations within the developing nations had been straightforward: Start from a low base and you can grow rapidly, with rates of growth easily surpassing those of the more heavily industrialized nations. Over time, you could catch up.

By the early 1980s, however, it had become obvious that many developing nations had shown no growth. In fact, says Botero, "an important group of countries were actually growing in negative terms. By the end of the 1970s they were registering per capita incomes lower than they had at independence 20 years before.

"So for those countries the situation was clear. They were never going to catch up; and, in fact, they were worse off than when the exercise started."

Botero's conclusion is clear: The old system of measurement was simply "an idea that led us in the wrong direction." In his view, the time is ripe for a new idea.

ह∙

In his decades of public life, Robert S. McNamara has retired from more high positions than most people ever dream of attaining: former chief executive of the Ford Motor Company, former Secretary of Defense, former president of the World Bank. He is, however, anything but retiring. Forthright without being rash, insistent but not obstreperous, he seasons his breadth of worldly experience with a deep concern for the moral dimensions of human behavior. Whether he agrees or disagrees, he does so squarely: You're never left guessing where he stands.

On this occasion, his agreement with Botero's interpretation is complete. "There isn't any real need to argue the point," he says with a shrug. "It's absolutely impossible, mathematically and economically, to significantly close the gap [for most nations] within the next fifty years. There's no way."

Estimates based on World Bank figures confirm his point: If current rates of growth continue, reaching parity with the industrial nations would take Thailand 365 years, the People's Republic of China 2,900 years, and Mauritania 3,224 years. To close the gap more rapidly, McNamara notes, would require the GNP of the developing nations to grow about 10 percent per year—again, something he considers impossible.

Is the situation hopeless? Not at all, says Botero. "I believe that if one is to offer goals for the future, they should be goals that can bring about hope," he says. "And the hopeful aspect of this relationship comes about if one changes the goal from closing the gap in absolute terms (in terms of dollars per capita per year) to a more simple one of finding ways of measuring human welfare other than in GNP per capita."

What, then, are some other ways of assessing the well-being of the world's nations?

Population. In 1950, one third of the world's people lived in industrialized nations. By the early decades of the 21st century, that number will be less than one sixth, as population pressures intensify in the developing world. Observers still debate the extent to which a large population, in and of itself, inhibits well-being: Even in the industrial world, densely packed Japan, with 824 people per square mile, has a more robust economy than that of sprawling Canada, with only 7 people per square mile. But in the developing world, high and rising populations, especially when coupled with poor economic performance, seem almost universally to discourage well-being.

Age. In the large group of developing nations that lie within the tropics, writes Peter Raven of the Missouri Botanical Garden, an average of 40 percent of the population is under fifteen. The corresponding figure for industrial nations is only 22 percent. Result: a built-in certainty of much more rapid growth rates in the tropics than in the northern nations, as this large population reaches child-bearing age.

Poverty. The World Bank estimates that some 40 percent of the 2.7 billion people in tropical and subtropical regions outside of China live in absolute poverty: they are unable to count on adequate food, clothing, and shelter from day to day. In those regions, according to UNICEF, more than fourteen million children under age five starve to death or die of disease each year, or nearly forty thousand a day.

Delivery of services. Many countries, including some with positive rates of growth in per capita income, are falling behind in meeting the demand for clean water, adequate nutrition, education, medical services, transportation, and communication.

There are, in other words, important measures of a nation's well-being other than per capita GNP. Some of these measures are trending downwards; but others are bright spots of hope. In China, Sri Lanka, and the Indian state of Kerala, for example, per capita GNP is still very low by Western standards, while other indicators (infant mortality, life expectancy, literacy, nutrition, employment, numbers living in poverty) show real progress.

What are the indicators that, separate from per capita GNP, give us an accurate picture of the well-being of a nation? Botero singles out four measures. Nations are doing well, he says, that exhibit:

- low infant mortality rate,
- widespread literacy,
- high life expectancy, and
- modest population growth.

Any nation that performs well according to these indicators, he argues, can be said to have a solid level of well-being, despite its comparative ranking along the GNP scale.

On the other hand, it is that very GNP scale that concerns British politician Shirley Williams. Questioning Botero's formulation with all the tact of a well-versed debater, she begins by agreeing. "I find the concept attractive," she emphasizes. Then she zeros in on three problems:

1. The disproportion between "the share of world resources going to the developed world compared to the developing world." That, she insists, "continues to be a serious problem": the 25 percent of the world's population living in the industrial world consumes some 82 percent of the world's resources.

2. The disproportion *within* developing countries among different income groups. In such countries as Brazil, Argentina, and Zaire, she says, there is a vast "internal differential" between the richest and the poorest segments of society. She recalls seeing a survey showing that in the past twelve years "the standard of living of the bottom half of the Brazilian people dropped by 32 percent, while the standard of living of the top 5 percent had increased by over 100 percent."

3. The need to "persuade the developed world to begin to shift resources, at least to some extent, back to the developing world." At present, she notes, the developing world is "losing resources to the developed world—not the other way around." Without that reversal, she says, "I don't think even Mr. Botero's modest ambitions will be achieved."

Her point: Whatever measures we choose, we must not overlook the necessity for providing adequate levels of economic activity within the developing nations, perhaps requiring the West to pay far more attention to the problem than it has in the recent past.

On that point, too, McNamara agrees. "I think we in the developed world have failed miserably," he says. Today, he explains, our real per capita income is twice what it was at the time of the Marshall Plan, measured "any way you want: beef consumption per capita, children in college, trips to Europe." Yet compared to that postwar period, "we have cut our development assistance in relation to income per capita by 90 percent."

Does that mean, then, that the industrial nations must share more of their wealth? Yes, says Botero—provided only that they are careful not to collapse their own economies in the process. "Some years ago," he notes, "the idea of zero growth became fashionable in certain circles. But after the oil shock [in 1973], the world had a few years of zero growth; and I don't think anybody liked it. One thing that is clear from that experience is that one of the worst things that can happen to the developing countries is for the industrialized countries to stagnate."

On that very point, however, Amitai Etzioni presses a question. "Is there," he asks, "a sociology of reallocation" that would allow a genuine redistribution of global resources and not simply produce a world having "a lot of people living longer with fewer resources"? He cites three possible ways forward, only the last of which he sees as viable:

Shifts in political power. "If the Third World could force the West or maybe the East to dislodge major resources, then there would be reallocation. That's what's known as revolution, and I don't think we would like the consequences."

New social movements. "If you had some mysterious social movement in the West—a kind of Zen Buddhism

22

where we would all enjoy sunsets—then we might be more willing to dislodge resources as we became less interested in material goods. But again, that's a fantasy."

Reduction of arms spending. Given that the world annually spends some $1 trillion on armaments, the resource available in this "third pocket," he says, is "not trivial." Nor is it localized in the industrial nations. "It's important to realize," says Etzioni, "that we're not talking about just the American-Soviet arms races. We're talking about the Pakistan-India arms race and all those other ones. So I think before we tell people that they have to live in their misery—more people, fewer resources—it deserves looking for one moment at those pockets spent on more killing.

"I grew up in the Middle East," Etzioni continues. "Islam and the Arab countries have been in it now for a long time. What happens each year? For the same old conflicts, we used to use handguns and hand grenades. Now they use superjets. Well, what have they achieved?"

He doesn't wait for an answer. His point is that the world is no better for the glut of weapons. Then why not a global arms cut?

Until recently, he says, that idea (the notion that arms could actually be reduced) was thought to be merely "a liberal or pacifist fantasy." But now that the Reagan-Gorbachev summit has produced an agreement for arms reduction, "maybe we are ready for a new world in which the superpowers, with some local collaboration, could get into the business of extinguishing local fires as they reduce their own arms races. Why does Argentina have to arm itself against Brazil and Brazil against Argentina before they come and talk to us about resources?"

He admits that, given the vigorous activity of global arms

merchants, "there's a long way to go." But, he concludes, "I don't want to leave [this discussion] on the notion that there's nothing to reallocate."

Down through the years, however, efforts at reallocation have generally failed, a point made by Gen. Olusegun Obasanjo, former head of state of Nigeria. He's no stranger to the reallocation of power. After turning over his nation to civilian rule in 1979, he returned to his farm near Abeokuta. In the years since, he has become one of the best known and most highly respected of his continent's internationalists. A quiet speaker whose gracious manner hides a puckish affection for humanity, he currently devotes much of his time to a small but influential organization, the New York-based Inter-Action Council, comprising other former heads of state. "We are not hamstrung by what I call the baggage of office," he points out, adding that these days, without the responsibility for heading national governments, "the world is our constituency."

Not surprisingly, Obasanjo is heartened by a sense of forward movement in matters of global development. "I know that we have made mistakes in the past," he says, "a lot of them. But up until now we were not even admitting that we had failed. Now we are admitting it, and I think maybe that is a beginning of success for us, limited as it may be.

"But if we have failed in the past," he asked, directing the question at his longtime acquaintance Robert McNamara, "what are the indications now that we will not fail again?"

"In this imperfect world," replies McNamara, "I am finally coming to the conclusion that each of us must assume responsibility for our own destiny. And that applies to nations. And the worst thing a developing country can do is say, 'It's all your fault, Mr. West or Mr. Developed Country: We've got to wait until you increase your resource flow to us before we can address the problems of our people.'

"I think we in the West are visibly immoral today in our attitudes toward the developing countries. But I don't think that's going to change quickly, not by the end of the century. And I do believe that the developing peoples and their leaders can help themselves."

How to help themselves? McNamara applauds those governments that have had the political will to take responsibility for their own development. Comparing Tanzania and Sri Lanka, for example, he notes that "Tanzania received far more financial resources from the external world than Sri Lanka, and it did far more poorly. Why? Because the political leadership had different goals and different effectiveness.

"I think one major point that needs to be made is that the primary responsibility for development rests not with some external force," he adds, but with a nation's "political leadership, its will, its moral objectives."

Those moral objectives, in fact, are central in determining a nation's response to the goals of development, which is why Botero longs to see the goals shift away from GNP and toward what he calls "levels of human welfare, levels of well-being, that are relatively simple and not necessarily ethnocentric, in that they don't necessarily imply the values of one society."

And that—the concern for preserving indigenous values—is, for many developing nations, a crucial issue. In ways that some northern nations have difficulty comprehending, the centuries-old question of values remains central in the South. Those nations often fear that the very kind of development that could lift them out of poverty might also destroy their cultures and traditions. Nazir Ahmad, a graduate student at Stanford University from Bangladesh, warns against "an element of interventionism" that comes when development projects bring Western values with them. "Maybe we need to create a little bit more isolationism in the West, to give us breathing room," he says.

Indian journalist and television filmmaker Vineet Narain agrees. "There is a need to focus our attention away from material values and toward the human," he says. The object, he says, should be the people themselves: "their welfare, their pleasure, their joy, and their spiritual and mental development.

"So far, it seems that most of the attention within the West has been on improving the material lot," he adds, noting the mistaken assumption that "this increases human welfare and joy." What is needed, he says, is "to restore people's faith in things which are traditional."

Kenyan journalist Patrick Mungai notes the bad impression left by cash-heavy development projects that failed. "We have in the Third World countries what are now popularly called 'white elephant projects,' projects that have been financed by the Western donors, where a lot of money has been poured in, but that can't function."

In addition to the public failures, he also calls attention to the private tragedies within families. "In my city, Nairobi, you find first-class residential areas; and half a mile away you find slums such as you have never seen. So what Mr. Botero said is very, very important to me. You read Kenya's GNP per capita, and every year the finance minister says it's rising. But the gap between the poor and the rich is widening."

All of which supports the case for measuring progress by something more meaningful than income. "Lowering the infant mortality rate," says Botero, "means much more to the ordinary man and woman of a developing country than obtaining an X percentage of growth in the GNP per capita, which to the majority of [those] people is an absolutely abstract and mysterious concept."

But there is another important reason for changing the way the gap is measured: Income figures can distort the perception of a nation's overall condition. A small country where the majority lives in poverty, but where a thin layer at the top possesses extravagant wealth, may show a high per capita income. But that, says Botero, "does not necessarily mean development.

"The twelve thousand dollars of income per capita of Saudi Arabia does not mean that Saudi Arabia's a developed country," he adds by way of example, noting that Saudi levels of literacy, infant mortality, and life expectancy are still well below the standards for the industrial nations. So the issue, he insists, is not one of *total* benefit but of *distribution* of that benefit across the entire society. And that leads him to an all-important point: When a country's progress is measured by something other than wealth, the results cannot mask a lack of distribution.

"You cannot lower the infant-mortality rate," says Botero, "unless you offer to *all* of the population a minimum of medical service, instead of offering it to the 10 percent wealthy urban elite. You cannot obtain 85 or 90 percent literacy rates in a society unless you offer primary education to the *whole* of your population, instead of offering very good education to 5 or 10 percent of the elite. You cannot achieve seventy years of life expectancy at birth unless you extend to *all* social classes minimum conditions of hygiene, nutrition, education, and literacy."

"But why would I *want* to do it?" interjects Shirley Williams, ever mindful of the political realities within the goal-setting process. "That's what puzzles me. I'm the Saudi Arabians. I've got money coming out of my ears, and I'm not going to accept your goals. There are an awful lot of governments that *don't* accept them. And what keeps troubling me is, How do you make governments accept those goals?"

The answer, says Botero, is to change the emphasis we put on various measures of well-being. Present-day indicators, based on income, "allow the Saudi Arabians to be proud in the world because they say, 'Look, we have twelve thousand dollars GNP per capita.' They're looking beautiful. They have a higher GNP, according to the standards we have set, than most of the Western European countries.

"But if we were using [these other measures], we'd say, 'Shut up! You have an infant mortality rate of one hundred per thousand, which is the infant mortality rate of a *fourth*-world country!' So at least you shame them."

ॐ

Perhaps you can shame nations into compliance—and perhaps you can't. The issue, however, goes far deeper than that. At bottom, the question is one of fairness, equity, and the distribution of resources across a broad spectrum. And that is exactly what intrigues Zhang Yi.

Listening to him, you might mistake Zhang for a young second-generation American of Chinese descent: His English, learned not so many years ago in British schools and honed in the American university system, is skilled and accurate. In fact, Zhang is a researcher at the Institute of American Studies, part of the Chinese Academy of Social Sciences in Peking. There, in a collegial, think-tank atmosphere unusual in his country, he is currently writing a book explaining the workings of the U.S. Congress to his compatriots.

An enthusiastic participant at Wingspread, he wrote later to say that "what impresses me most about the conference is that it shows very clearly that there are people who care not only about their own personal problems, but also the problems facing the whole of mankind. I believe such caring on the part of more members of the world community is absolutely essential to the survival of our planet."

Zhang's caring—which balances his Western training against the long tradition of social welfare in China—produced a statement both memorable and encouraging. Speaking to the issue of equity and distribution, Zhang puts it simply. His point is that, on this issue, different countries may need to take different paths.

"For some countries," he says, citing the standard Marxist approach, "where there is a high degree of wealth polarization, there should be an effort to redistribute the wealth."

But his next observation indicates the depth of the rethinking occurring in the world's most populous Communist nation—or at least among Zhang's colleagues. "In countries where there is too much equality, which I think there is in China, there should be more stratification, there should be people who should be richer. There should be some degree of inequality, as long as those inequalities will help the least well off in the society."

Then, returning to Williams's question about whether nations will be willing to change their scales of measurement, he notes that "you can't *make* the developing countries accept the goals." Acceptance, he adds, "really depends on the internal, political interaction inside the particular country itself."

British columnist Katharine Whitehorn agrees. "None of these indicators will really work unless you consider their relation to the social structure in which they are working," she says. The problem, she suggests, is that "we are trying to look for something which you can measure; and most of the things that matter *cannot* be measured. The reason we've grasped GNP is because it's so easy to measure.

"Let's get back to the one thing, absolute poverty, and stick to that," she continues, "because everything else is going to vary from country to country and region to region."

But how, asks General Obasanjo, do you measure absolute poverty?

"Well, people dying of starvation would do fairly well, wouldn't it?" she replies.

"There are many people who are not dying of starvation," counters the General, "but they are on the verge of starvation. They are not getting two square meals a day. Are they absolutely poor?"

Yes indeed, agrees Whitehorn. If, on the other hand, life expectancy is used as the measure, the indicator may not really reflect a nation's well-being. "You may live for a long time in a desperate condition," she notes, "but you might in fact be worse off than somebody with a shorter life."

All of which, to futurist Ted Gordon, is well and good, although it doesn't address the need for some measure of economic well-being. "GNP is a very narrow, unidimensional measure," he says, noting that "it addresses only one aspect of the economy and does not address distribution at all." But some economic measures, he insists, are vital.

His proposal: consider adding some measure of employment. "Employment somehow captures a vitality, an economic vitality and a distributional measure as well," he points out.

"Ted just made my point," interjects Michael Hooker, president of the University of Maryland at Baltimore County. "The purpose of development capital was to put a country on its own feet. If you focus just on the indices of infant mortality and the other quality-of-life indices that you've suggested, it may be that we can raise all of those indices but never put a country on its feet. If we focus on something like employment, we can't avoid putting a country on its own feet."

But what is meant, he is asked, by "putting a country on its own feet"?

"Well, you want the country to be developmentally sufficient after a while," he explains. "You don't want it to be dependent on the developed nations forever for its quality of life. So you want investment capital to get the economy of the country moving. And one index of your having done that is that you've got employment increasing."

But will shifting to a new five-part set of goals (measuring infant mortality, population, adult literacy, life expectancy, and employment) really make a difference? The answer, according to Botero, is not at all clear, and for good reason. "Today," he notes, "these are not goals in the international community. Very few developing countries are deliberately seeking these goals; and, in fact, very many of them don't even track those indicators. But you first have to have goals in order to start achieving them."

Increasingly, however, such indicators are being sought across the world, a point Obasanjo makes. "Indicators such as wholesome drinking water, nutrition, education, health: we just cannot run away from them, because if those things are there, then the absoluteness of poverty will be removed." Countries that do well on such indicators, he adds, "may not be wealthy, but they will not be poor."

Yet isn't some measure of *absolute* wealth necessary in order for these other indicators to improve? No, says Botero, who points to countries as different as Barbados, Chile, Costa Rica, Cuba, and South Korea. None has a high level of per capita GNP. They have very different political systems. Yet each has managed to reach high levels of well-being as measured by literacy, infant mortality, and life expectancy.

"It is *not* a fact," insists McNamara, carving the air with his hand for emphasis, "that a country cannot achieve the levels of quality of life that Rodrigo [Botero] pointed to without high GNP. It is just not a fact. Mexico and Brazil have incomes per capita of five to ten times that of China; and on the measures that Rodrigo gave, they have lower levels [of well-being].

"Don't misunderstand me," he adds. "I'm not opposed to

31

growth. I think we should include among Rodrigo's items a moderate increase in GNP per capita. But the point is that unless the government wishes to insure that [GNP growth] is used to benefit the mass of the people, it won't be. Growth does not bring quality of life: Quality of life can be achieved without high income levels."

Kristin Helmore, a journalist specializing in developing-world issues who has traveled widely and written extensively on the subject for *The Christian Science Monitor,* agrees. "I don't feel that the fulfillment of [Botero's] goals excludes an increase in GNP," she observes. "I think the second would follow from the first, because in developing countries there is an extremely vital informal sector which is often cramped by ill health caused by malnutrition."

It follows, she says, that "if people have a more healthy living standard, they will get on with the business that they are already involved in. There is no one who is unemployed in the developing country: They would die of starvation if they didn't do something. So it seems to me that it's not an either/or choice between GNP or these goals, but these goals would further the GNP growth."

Money, then, may not be the only answer. But there is widespread agreement among those around the table that it's a necessary part of the solution. North-South development must still depend in part on capital. But the measurable, attainable goals for the year 2000 should be something other than raw wealth.

"Let us try to center on things that are fundamental for having a decent society," concludes Botero, "even if it's not rich."

Chapter 3

East-West Relations

Ask Gail Lapidus to characterize the present moment in East-West relations and she puts it bluntly: enormous peril and outstanding opportunity.

It's a moment her entire career has prepared her to appreciate. Trained as a political scientist, she gravitated toward Soviet studies out of a conviction that the management of East-West relations in the nuclear age is, as she puts it, "the critical issue for the survival not only of our respective societies but of the entire universe." Accustomed to tracking the give-and-take of superpower negotiations, she is well prepared to assess the storms of argument that swirl across that diplomatic horizon, and equally ready to jump into a roundtable on Soviet issues with a quiver full of examples and an absorbed interest in the target.

Lapidus is no ideologue. When the phrase "achieving peace" surfaces in our discussions, she quickly disassociates herself from it. "That suggests to me a one-time achievement," she explains, "something that you can capture and will then forever after be in possession of." Instead, she observes, "the task of avoiding nuclear war and of shaping a more stable and cooperative East-West relationship is something that has to be worked on constantly, a process rather than an objective." Just now, she says, that process is producing an entirely new pattern in East-West relations. "This is an extraordinarily important moment. It may indeed be a watershed, a point from which it may become possible to take a whole series of very constructive steps which could lead to a major reduction of tensions and a much more stable international environment in the years and decades ahead."

Why? Because "Soviet behavior has been the most significant source and propellant for some of the major international tensions of the mid-twentieth century," she explains. "This is not to suggest that American and Western behavior, and the behavior of other actors, haven't contributed to the problems that we face. And I'm also not suggesting that there aren't other sources of international tension that are quite independent of the Soviet Union. But I do assume that there are certain characteristics of Soviet behavior in the international environment that have been a significant source of major international tensions."

Logically, then, she concludes that "a change in the nature of Soviet international behavior could make a significant contribution toward changing the international environment." And that's exactly what she now sees happening. The Soviet Union, she explains, is undergoing "what we might almost call a normalization," in which "some of its most abhorrent and most aberrant features are being reduced."

What's the nature of that "normalization"? It involves, in the first place, a change in values. Under the *perestroika* ("restructuring") initiated by Gorbachev, she says, there is "a major struggle" under way, involving "a change in the values of the key segment within the Soviet elite." The change entails what she calls "a revival of the more humanistic strands of socialism after their extinction during Stalin's period," coupled with "an effort to de-legitimize key features of Stalinism, particularly its brutality, its more criminal aspects."

The shift in values also involves the dawning of "a form of Socialist pluralism: a rejection of the notion that there is a single truth, and an acceptance of the need for a variety of points

34

of view." Taking form in a more diverse social structure, this change, she says, tends toward "a repudiation of the notion of the homogeneous society" and toward "a recognition that there are social differences, group differences, ethnic differences that are not only legitimate but even desirable, and that contribute an element of richness and diversity to the human community." Out of this new sense of diversity grows "a degree of tolerance"—a new phenomenon, she says, which "marks a decisive end to a regime which for long periods of time has conducted warfare against its own people."

Along with this growth in humanism, pluralism, and tolerance comes a second set of changes, involving power. Recent Soviet moves suggest "a trend toward greater dispersion of power: dispersion of economic power in the form of marketization, and the dispersion of political power with the campaign for greater democratization." Both moves, she says, tend toward "a system which is more responsive to the needs and interests of the population," one in which "officials are more accountable for their actions."

A third trend, she says, involves the effect of *glasnost* ("openness"). She sees in today's Soviet society "a less xenophobic attitude toward the outside world," coupled with "a less frightened attitude toward its own population." Beginning to crumble, she says, is "the excessive secrecy of the Soviet system, the effort to create Iron Curtains and barriers, the insulation from the outside world."

As changes occur in these three areas (values, power, and openness), the implications for foreign policy are profound. In particular, Lapidus sees:

A changing definition of security. The Soviet elite is moving away from "the notion of security as a zero sum relationship, in which a diminution of someone else's security automatically leads to an increase in yours." In its place, she says, is a recognition that "the Soviet Union will not be more secure if it succeeds in making its neighbors feel less secure."

A lessening reliance on military power. Flowing from changing views of security is "a recognition that power should not be defined so narrowly and exclusively in military terms, but has a much broader dimension, that it is a function of economic strength, a function of political efficacy, a function of the appeal of one's values and one's country to a larger constituency."

An increasing recognition of global interdependence. Soviet society is slowly shifting away from "the old Leninist conception of the world as fundamentally divided and in fundamental conflict, the notion of world revolution as very much a we-versus-they process." Replacing that conception is a realization of the need for global cooperation in addressing common problems, particularly the problem of nuclear armaments. As evidence, she cites "an increasing emphasis on the elements of cooperation" within the Soviet Union, coupled with "an increasing tendency to downplay or subordinate those elements that are adversarial or conflictual."

The result is an increased willingness on the part of other nations to integrate the Soviet Union into the larger international community. That, in turn, has led to a new appreciation, on the part of the Soviets, of the role of the United Nations "as an instrument for conciliation and integration." It has also engendered a growing willingness by the Soviets "to become involved with other political systems in political and cultural and scientific exchanges on a scale that goes far beyond anything that has ever been contemplated."

A growing respect for international diversity. "Instead of treating the existence of different political, social, ideological, and economic systems as a source of danger and of confrontation," says Lapidus, "you're beginning to get in some recent Soviet speeches and statements the notion that that diversity may in fact be an advantage." With this attitude comes "a greater willingness to tolerate diversity within the Socialist Bloc itself." The result: major changes in the Soviet attitude toward China, along with "a recognition that the different paths adopted by different countries in Eastern Europe in the development of socialism may have something to contribute to the Soviet Union." Overall, she says, these changes constitute "a very sharp repudiation of the earlier notion that the Soviet Union presented the model which all other countries had to imitate."

Recognition of the importance of trust. Soviets increasingly see their relations with other nations as requiring some element of trust. So far, she says, that has involved "a willingness—in some still very early, very limited degree—to sacrifice some degree of secrecy." Sharing information about Chernobyl and inviting groups of U.S. congressmen and scientists to visit military installations are signs, she feels, of an effort to "break down some of the elements of secrecy and mistrust that have been such obstacles to international cooperation."

Lapidus is quick to point out, however, that "all of these trends are still very embryonic." She emphasizes that there is "a major struggle going on in the Soviet Union," the outcome of which is "impossible to predict." Barring major setbacks or a defeat of the reform process, however, these trends "carry with them an enormous potential, the potential to make the Soviet Union a more constructive participant in the global arena in ways that we have not seen before."

Those, then, are the features of East-West relations that suggest the "outstanding opportunities" for a safer, saner world. But what about the "enormous peril"?

Shuichi Kato speaks to that. With his tweed-and-sweater apparel, his slightly flyaway hair, and his sober features flecked with the hints of smiles, he exudes the aura of a world-class academician whose visiting professorships have taken him from his native Japan to universities in America, West Germany, and Mexico. A former medical doctor who turned to poetry, fiction, and journalism fairly late in his career, he now travels widely. In the taxi from the airport to Wingspread, in fact, he talked expansively about his insights into some of the Soviet Bloc countries, gathered from a just-concluded speaking tour in Eastern Europe.

It is that subject to which he turns as, contemplating what Lapidus has said, he explores some of the perils of East-West relations. He worries that, for Eastern Europe, *perestroika* contains some "built-in contradictions." Noting that "the new policy implies more freedom of maneuver for Eastern European countries," he comments that such freedom is generally thought to lead toward greater openness, and "even to integration into the West."

But will that be the case? Given prevalent poverty and hunger, he says, a socialist nation granted more freedom might be expected to turn westward. Such, however, is "not necessarily the present situation in Czechoslovakia or in East Germany." In those countries, more freedom for the government appears to mean more ability to mount strong resistance toward the newfound openness, a new freedom to resist the very changes that might otherwise undermine the authority and privilege of the governing elite.

The impact of *glasnost,* however, is not limited to Soviet bloc nations. Stella Maria, a trade unionist from Indonesia, notes that already "the effect of *glasnost*" is being felt in her country. Many Third World countries, she says, have long espoused the principles of democracy, based on Western examples. But "we do not really implement them," she notes, explaining that the result has been a kind of "artificial democracy."

Now, however, "when we demand openness and more democracy, people say, 'We can't do without it—because even the Soviet Union is getting it!' I think this might be a very positive influence toward the Third World countries," she adds, noting that the concept of *glasnost* is already part of "our daily talk in Indonesia."

These examples confirm a point central to Lapidus's thesis: that the ultimate effects of current Soviet changes are varied, difficult to foresee, and even more difficult to influence.

"I start from the assumption that it is not within our power [in the West] to significantly affect outcomes within the Soviet Union," she says. The outside world, she admits, does exert powerful indirect influences through political and economic models. "But these are rather indirect processes" which don't have any "immediate impact on Soviet outcomes."

"But if the reform is in our interest," asks Obasanjo, "is there really absolutely nothing we can do to encourage the reform to succeed in the interest of a better future for all of us?"

"We know so little about the internal Soviet scene," replies Lapidus, "that it's very difficult to know whether measures that we might think would be helpful might not indeed turn out to be hurtful. In other words, I think that our knowledge is much too limited for it to be wise to risk any major effort to intervene, because the outcome would be very unpredictable. Suppose you took some steps that you thought were going to help Gorbachev, which have the effect of galvanizing his opposition into the argument that he is a stooge of the West. All these things can backfire: It's a very delicate political situation."

Regardless of the risk, one goal that many observers would like to set is greater East-West dialogue. For Meinhard Ade, director general of the office of President Richard von Weizsäcker in West Germany, the reduction of the sense of antagonism between East and West is "a really important goal [for] the year 2000."

Reflecting on the Cold War years, Ade says that "the competition between Eastern and Western systems was not a competition that gave us force." Instead, it was a "paralyzing" competition that prevented both sides from addressing "more important questions."

In the future, he asks, will Europe "react to events in the Soviet Union with an attitude to help them, or will we continue with our strategy of the last twenty years to have [merely] a coexistence?" Ade argues that Europe's best interest lies in the former course. By way of example, he notes that events in the Soviet Union can have immediate impact on Poland or East Germany, resulting in "a hundred thousand or a hundred fifty thousand Polish [citizens] immigrating to [West Germany]." The goal for the year 2000, he says, is "not to be pessimistic and not to be optimistic" about the Soviet system, but simply to "be clear that we have to help."

Nigerian journalist John Araka, agreeing that more dialogue is needed, extends the issue to include more communication in general, not only between the nations now holding the most threatening weapons, but among all the world's nations. Putting the present situation in historical perspective, he notes that "at the beginning of this century, nobody knew that the United States and the Soviet Union would acquire the type of weaponry that can destroy mankind." Nor, he adds, can we now foresee which nations might have similar weaponry by the middle of the next century.

One thing, however, is clear: Today "there are very many other countries, even in the so-called Third World, that have developed their own nuclear capabilities." If that trend continues, "some countries that today are irrelevant in the calculations of the world may become very important: they may be the people to determine whether or not there should be peace in the world.

"If we want to achieve peace in a nuclear age in the next century, the emphasis really should be on communication," Araka continues. Why? Because "as more and more nations acquire nuclear technology without necessarily improving their economic systems, such countries can turn out to be very dangerous in the future, because, out of frustration, out of annoyance, they can press the button."

For Ted Gordon, former aerospace engineer, such proliferation represents "the most threatening" aspect of nuclear weaponry in the next century. And, he stresses, "it's very difficult to solve. To control it, industrial nations typically must deny technology to developing nations—a highly unpopular stance."

Dangerous as it may be, nuclear proliferation is not the only problem. "I think we should recognize that technology which is currently in the laboratory or beyond the laboratory is also potentially destabilizing. Chemical and biological weapons take on a new dimension in the next century in terms of their ease of production and their threatening strategic implications." This is particularly true, Gordon says, of genetically-based weapons, for they target particular races.

The proliferation of weaponry may represent, as Gordon suggests, a specific future threat. For many around our table, however, there has already been a significant movement toward another, more general proliferation: that of power. What is gradually evolving is a view of global security that goes far beyond the classic struggle between two superpowers.

"There aren't superpowers now," asserts Shirley Williams. Tracing the concept of a superpower to the post-World War II years, she notes that in 1945 the United States produced 70 percent of the gross national product of the West. "Today, she produces 22 percent of the world's GNP and 9.5 percent of the world's trade," says Williams. "America is no longer economically the superpower. Nor is the Soviet Union."

Then why continue to speak of "superpower" relations? "It's just that none of the rest of us," she says, "have raised our voices loud enough to say, 'Excuse me, the emperor's got no clothes!' because we're frightened the emperor might be cross." In fact, she points out, "the Germans have got more clothes than the Americans, and so have the Japanese. And, for that matter, when it comes to the Soviet Union, East Germany is a proportionately more powerful economy than the Soviet Union. But who dares to say so?"

The emperor may indeed have no clothes. But "the other formulation," quips former Arms Control Agency official Adam Yarmolinsky, our moderator, is that "there is no emperor in those clothes."

ॐ

Yarmolinsky's jibe has point: The clothing the superpowers still do possess (their nuclear weaponry) is the one thing that should raise alarms across the rest of the world. Yet the alarms are not often sounded loudly—a fact that puzzles some onlookers.

One of the more perplexed is American ecologist William C. Clark. A slender, youthful-looking man, whose expressive face is set off by an oddly clerical combination of dark turtleneck and light open-collared shirt, he's spent the last three years at the International Institute for Applied Systems Analysis in Austria, an institution set up by the Soviet Union, the

United States, Japan, West Germany, and fifteen other countries to examine what he calls "these big cross-cutting international issues" that connect science and politics.

Interested in "long-term interactions between environmental change and economic developments," he recently moved to the Kennedy School of Government at Harvard, "where ecologists don't belong," he chuckles, but where there's some hope for finding ways to bring scientific and economic knowledge together with "the people who are committing themselves to lives in public service and performance." A specialist by training but a generalist by instinct, he sets no limits to his intellectual interests and no bounds to the sense of moral urgency he brings to the discussions at hand.

"I've been surprised, almost stunned, at the lack of expression of a sense of moral outrage on this issue of security and peace," he begins. "We've been discussing it as though it were a blemish in our economic performance, something that hasn't quite gone right and we have to fix it. We've not been discussing it in the sense that the stocks of weapons we now have so clearly hang the specter of absolute annihilation over us, and that we have done this to ourselves! We do not talk about it in terms of the incredible drain that the annual flows of expenditures on military and so-called security issues impose upon us in every single society we're talking about.

"Now, I think we've seen in the last several years — perhaps particularly in Europe, but in many other areas as well — a sense of how powerful that moral outrage can be, a sense of the kind of impetus and pressure it can put on individuals and governments for change."

Needed just now, he continues, is more effort "to think about ways of amplifying and channeling that moral outrage into effective channels for demanding actions everywhere, from our own individual levels as citizens up through and focusing on the level of our leaders."

Robert McNamara agrees that such focusing is needed. The one obvious channel for it, he says, is the United Nations. But the UN, in his view, has not worked. Why? "For just one very simple reason. It hasn't functioned because the United States and the Soviet Union haven't permitted it to. That's the problem.

"Now, there is a high probability that if the United States and the Soviet Union worked together, you could create the United Nations as a major force in the world for peace-keeping in a nuclear age. Gorbachev has indicated his willingness to do so. That ought to be a major goal for the twenty-first century."

McNamara also suggests that nations other than the superpowers have larger roles to play. "It is disgraceful that we sit around this table and you nations—non-U.S., non-Soviet—have not gone to the UN and said, 'This is an issue of morality. It is an issue of legality. You have put our nations at risk. If you ever carry out your NATO and Warsaw Pact strategy, you're going to destroy yourselves. Up until recently we thought if you were stupid enough to pursue [such] a strategy, that was your problem. [But now] we are learning that through climatic conditions you will destroy *us*. We will not tolerate that. We wish you to present to us a verifiable agreement that, starting next year or certainly in the twenty-first century, you will no longer put our nations at risk. It's immoral. It's illegal. We won't tolerate it!'"

What McNamara is speaking of, in fact, is yet another example of global interdependence, the new reality in international affairs that gives special vitality to the moral issues he raises. Yet global interdependence is a concept with which some nations are uneasy, as Radcliffe president Matina Horner observes. "We have an enormous capacity, even though we use the *word,* to deny the *fact* of interdependence," she says. The reason, she explains, is that nations fear that "it may suggest a weakening of power or independence."

She sees the need for a new set of guidelines. What, she asks, are going to be "the rules for relating under an interdependent network—whether it's between men and women, between groups within our own country, or between the first and the Third World—that are different from the rules that govern relationships if we continue to see independent and dependent beings, first powers and secondary powers?

"Unless we grapple with that and help people really understand it—not just *say* it but really *understand* it—we'll never get away from the capacity to dehumanize others who are different from ourselves, whether that be by gender or color or religion or political ideology." That very dehumanizing, she insists, permits humanity "to entertain proliferation of nuclear, biological, or chemical warfare, or to ignore ecological impacts."

The need, she concludes, is to "get away from *we/they* to an *us.*"

One way to build on such interdependence, says Clark, is by creating new forums for interaction. Noting that international forums exist for the discussion of economic matters, he suggests the creation of "analogous forums of world leaders addressed to the issue of world security.

"We have built international economic summits for talking periodically about economic prosperity," he says. While they serve as forums for the exchange of ideas, they "also serve a function of accountability. The leaders of many of the larger nations have got to come together and walk out of those summits exposed to [such questions as], 'What have you accomplished? Have you left the problems in the same miserable state they were in when you walked into the summit? Or can you at least manufacture some image that a little step forward has been taken?'"

For Clark, a "reasonable objective for the next ten years" would be the creation of some similar forum of world leaders that "could hold them to account" for answering such questions as, "What have you done to reduce the annual expenditure per capita this year on arms? What have you done in the last two years to reduce the standing stocks [of armaments]?'" He would prefer to see such a security summit made into "a focal point, so that the world just howls at these people, domestically and internationally, if progress is not made. I think we've got to think in terms of mechanisms of this sort that can provide—in a media-conscious, image-conscious world—a way to go."

Those mechanisms, furthermore, should not just center on the large nations. They should be "systematically designed to provide a world stage on which we can't just pass off the responsibility and the guilt to the superpowers. The non-aligned nations—the Indias, the Colombias—would have to also say, 'What have *we* done this year to exert pressure on the superpowers? What have *we* done within our own governments to reduce these expenditures, to increase global security?'"

Can such mechanisms be established? The process, says Williams, has already begun. "We have two reports, the Brundtland Report and the Brandt Report, which said exactly what we need to do in the most radical terms. The Brandt Report couldn't have set it out more clearly. It said that every year there should be a one percent reduction in international flows of money on arms, which should be redirected towards the developing world. It came closer than anything else in our recent history to actually giving the world a new agenda. And we had in 1987 the Brundtland Report. It couldn't have set out more clearly the destruction of the world's environment, the need to take another look, the need to move very rapidly towards taking steps that would indeed stop the runaway series of demands on the world's resources.

"So we don't have to sit around, actually, and *think*. We've got these two statements before us. We're not going to do much better than that. The question that we have to address is, Why did nothing happen after those two reports? And the answer is that the entire political process is increasingly directed towards a very short-term response to public pressures for immediate gratifications in the West, and a very short-term response to a desire to achieve national expressions of achievement in the Third World. We haven't got away from the tyranny of the pursuit of nationalism on the one side and the pursuit of short-term material aggrandizement on the other."

For Williams, the answer lies along the lines of Clark's proposed creation of new forums. The need of the hour, she feels, is for "a forum which is driven by public opinion itself."

But public opinion is a broad-gauge thing, quite unlike the opinion of the narrow, well-educated elites typically involved in the foreign-policy process around the world. To expand that base will require a significant education process. And that, says Patrick Mungai, is nowhere more true than in the United States.

A senior editor with Kenya's largest newspaper, *The Daily Nation,* Mungai comes from a country so diverse and polyglot that, while he and his wife share one language in common, their children must use a language he himself doesn't know when they talk to their maternal grandparents. An uncommon mix of peaceful affability and bubbling curiosity, he is not particularly given to criticism, especially of his hosts. So his comments on America, largely the fruit of an extended visit as a fellow of the World Press Institute in 1984, come not out of rancor but well-meaning reflection, and testify both to the significance of the United States as a model to developing nations and to the efforts the U.S. must make to keep pace with an increasingly interdependent age.

"I have realized that if we are to achieve peace in the 21st century," says Mungai, "the American people must change their way of thinking. And if they're to change their way of thinking, then they must start by restructuring their education system. It appears to me that the American education system instills into very young minds that whatever is American is good. So this has made most Americans grow into adults who believe that they cannot borrow [any ideas] from an outside society.

"I believe that if we have to achieve some level of peace by the 21st century, the American people must be willing to learn from other societies. And this brings me to this *glasnost* concept in Russia. It appears that the Americans are receiving it with open hands, saying, 'Oh, the Russians, it has taken the Russians this long to realize that our system is good!' But they forget that they too can have a lot to learn from the Russian system.

"The only way the American people can know this is to start teaching their children that they can also learn something from other societies," he concludes. If that happens, he says, "these children, when they become decision makers, will be able to respect the views of other societies."

Such newfound respect would clearly enhance the prospects for stronger relations among nations. Vineet Narain takes the point a step farther. His goal: better relations among the various social groups *within* nations, especially in the developing world.

The new rules of intercommunication, he says, should not be confined only to Nairobi, Bombay, and other large Third

World cities. "People living in cities, even in the Third World, think the way Westerns do," he says. But "the majority of the population in Third World lives in rural areas. They understand things more rationally, and they are more down to earth." For him, the differences between city-dwellers and their rural cousins within a single nation are sometimes much greater than those between urban residents in entirely different cultures and require much more bridge-building.

One way to encourage such bridge-building, says American rural community organizer Billie Jean Young, is to "try, when we bring people together [from different nations], to bring together rural people, to bring together women, to bring together the people who are left out of governmental policies and the making of governmental policies." Most international gatherings, by contrast, bring together upper-level opinion leaders, usually from urban areas. Bringing together rural citizens from various nations, she says, might provide significant opportunities for learning, especially because they would come from "similar experiences and similar places in the social and economic strata."

American cognitive psychologist Edwin Hutchins agrees. "The point I want to make is somewhat puny," he says, "but I'm going to go ahead and make it anyway. Gail [Lapidus] pointed out some of the problems that the Soviet Union faces because they've not told themselves the truth about their own country. I think the whole planet faces a similar problem. We have to come to tell ourselves the truth."

The challenge, he says, lies not only among "the kind of people who are in this room, not just the leaders of the world or even the literate audiences of the newspapers. I think we really have to get to the grass roots and somehow instill a new sense of the circumstances of our species on this planet as we approach the end of this century.

"I'm struck by what most Americans seem to know about

the Third World. I think a lot of what Americans know they don't get from newspapers. They get it from popular media—films and television. Typically in those settings cultural diversity is not depicted as alternative ways for humans to exist. It's reduced to some kind of cultural exotica and stereotypes. I think the same thing is true within our own country in the way we depict various segments of our own society. So I would put as a goal—because we do need to get a wider sense of what our circumstances are—to get the media to seriously engage its moral responsibility to educate as well as to entertain."

But how will we measure the success of that education—or, for that matter, of any effort to resolve the East-West conflict and create a more peaceful world? For several of the participants, the answer lies in developing new standards for assessing peace. Bill Clark, noting that Rodrigo Botero suggested new measures for assessing the relationship of developing and industrial nations, observes that it would be useful to "think hard about some good, useful indicators of improving the security picture."

"I like the idea," says Ted Gordon. "I want to emphasize it since it was covered so quickly." Just as the *Bulletin of Atomic Scientists* has developed its "doomsday clock" indicating the proximity of a nuclear war, he explains, so "it would be very useful to have measures of peace.

"As far as I know," he continues, that clock is "the only measure we have. It's completely qualitative. But why not develop a set of measures, with a parallel to economic measures, that somehow indicate stability or proximity to peace? That, I think, is a very useful goal."

Chapter 4

Environmental Degradation

There's nothing ostentatious about George Woodwell's home. Set on a back street in Woods Hole, Massachusetts, the house at first glance seems typical of this part of Cape Cod: graciously aging, comfortably spacious, slightly drafty, and fronting an oceanside road where winter winds howl. There is, however, one unique feature. Across the driveway, where other people might have built a garage, the Woodwell family has constructed an odd-looking building several stories tall. Its front wall, sloping gently toward the roof, faces south and is sheathed in glass panels: a homemade solar collector, Dr. Woodwell explains. Except for the very coldest months of the New England winter, it heats the whole house and provides ample hot water.

For an ecologist dedicated to environmental issues, the house is perfectly in character. It allows him, in a personal way, to address what he sees as the overarching and impersonal problem of the next century: the global warming trend produced largely by the burning of fossil fuels.

It's a subject with which he's thoroughly conversant. An avuncular figure, his button-down collar, rough tweed jackets, and high forehead could fit him perfectly to a professorial life. He has, in fact, held academic positions at the University of Maine, Yale University, Brookhaven National Laboratory, and the Marine Biological Laboratory at Woods Hole. He now directs the Woods Hole Research Center, a small ecological organization center which increasingly draws environmentalists, politicians, diplomats, and reporters from across the globe.

There's a kind of fire in the belly that carries Woodwell beyond the merely intellectual approach. Environmental degradation is far more to him than an inconvenience, a blemish on man's record, or an economic hardship. It's a call to commitment. Building a solar collector, organizing an international conference: Whatever the task, in his view, the need of the hour is for action rather than simply more study. Why? Because, in the last few decades, something significant has changed. "Until now," he told the group at Wingspread, "the environment has been large in proportion to the demands that we've put on it. Now our influences are large."

What are those influences? They include pollution of global water supplies, increases in toxic wastes, expansion of the world's deserts, the destruction of the ozone layer, and the extinction of entire species of plant and animal life, all linked closely to a burgeoning global population. Some of these issues have immediate and tangible consequences, and, as a result, direct and local solutions. The call for clean water, for example, unites environmentalists, public health specialists, and economists around the world, especially those working in Third World nations. "If you could tomorrow morning make water clean in the world," says Bill Clark, "you would have done, in one fell swoop, the best thing you could have done for improving human health by improving environmental quality."

Woodwell does not disagree. But for him, as for many environmentalists, the knottiest problem (the one carrying the most long-range and least understood threat) is the global warming trend. Popularly known as "the greenhouse effect," it appears to be caused by an increase of carbon dioxide

52

(CO_2) and other gasses in the earth's atmosphere. Like greenhouse windows, the CO_2 lets the sun's rays through, and then traps the heat inside.

"Over the past century," Woodwell explains, "the composition of the atmosphere has increased by roughly 30 percent in its content of carbon dioxide. At the moment, the atmosphere contains about seven hundred billion tons of carbon. It's increasing annually at about three billion tons, including carbon from the combustion of fossil fuels, carbon from the destruction of forests, and probably carbon from the destruction of soils as the earth warms.

"Now, in saying that, I said a lot. The earth *is* warming. It's five tenths to seven tenths of a degree warmer now than it was about a century ago. Five of the warmest years in this last century have occurred in this decade, in the 1980s. There is abundant other evidence that appears to confirm the warming trend."

According to Woodwell, the seven hundred billion tons of atmospheric carbon has increased by about 25 percent in the past century. And it continues to increase, largely because the burning of fossil fuels releases about five billion tons of carbon annually. Perhaps half of that gets reabsorbed into the oceans. But an additional increment (he conservatively estimates half a billion tons, though it could be as high as four billion tons) comes from deforestation. How does deforestation compound the problem? Because, he explains, forest plants contain carbon, which, when they die and decay, is released as CO_2. In addition, he says, the photosynthesis that occurs in living forests consumes large amounts of CO_2, a process that stops when the forests are cut down.

Making things worse is the fact that the warming trend itself exacerbates the problem. "The warming increases the rate of decay of organic matter," he notes, explaining that "a one-degree warming can be expected to increase the rate of decay by somewhere between 5 percent to perhaps 20 or 30 percent, depending on where one is and the circumstance." The result: even more carbon dioxide released, as decaying forests grow ever warmer.

Taken together, these "physical factors" (burning of fossil fuels) and "biotic factors" (involving changes in forestation) account for the net annual accumulation of three billion tons of atmospheric carbon. He admits, however, that the scientific assessment of the biotic factors rests on "somewhat soft ground, because there really isn't objective data to separate out what the biotic contributions are." Part of the problem: the lack of a global appraisal of the extent of deforestation— easily attainable using satellite imagery, but yet to be undertaken.

Despite the uncertainties, however, scientists expect the extent of the warming to range between 1.5 and 5.5 degrees centigrade, corresponding, he says, to "the equivalent of a doubling of the carbon dioxide content of the atmosphere, expected to be achieved probably by 2030 or so." The change of temperature would be greatest at the middle and high latitudes, and greater in winter than in summer.

What would that do to agriculture? Such changes would inevitably produce a "migration" of vegetation zones of some sixty to one hundred miles north for every degree of temperature change. "So a degree change in a decade (which is possible in certain places in the higher latitudes) is really big stuff."

Woodwell observes that, although agriculture might well adapt to these changes, "the adaptations are bound to be painful." The change would also include the further destruction of forests, as certain species of trees could no longer survive in once-forested areas. If even a half-degree shift in temperature over a decade wipes out forests, he says, "we don't have the potential for remaking those forests elsewhere, at least not that rapidly. And that results in an additional release of carbon."

Also affected would be sea levels, which could rise by as much as seven feet by the year 2100 due to melting of the polar ice caps. At present rates of warming, he says, "there's not much question that we could open up the Arctic Ocean, which is now frozen." That ocean is currently "a reflective white body" which bounces sunlight back into the atmosphere. If melted, however, it would absorb even more of the sun's heat, further increasing the warming trend and causing unpredictable climatic changes. "You just don't play with that sort of unpredictable circumstance in a world that's trying to squeeze ten billion people into itself," he says.

Nor do you write off such warnings as merely speculative. "We are almost certainly committed," he says, "to a substantial warming of the earth. If we continue on the current course, emitting enough carbon to result in a three-billion-ton-per-year addition to what's in the atmosphere now, we shall be entering a period of indefinite warming, indefinite climatic change, and leaving a period of comparatively stable climates over the past centuries. And an open-ended warming is just not really something we can live with."

What, then, is to be done? "I see little alternative to reducing that buildup of carbon dioxide in the atmosphere to zero," he concludes. "You really do have to stabilize the composition of the atmosphere and stabilize climates globally if we wish to continue to use the earth effectively."

For many environmentalists, the way forward is as obvious as it is uncomfortable: Cut back the global use of fossil fuels. A 50 percent decrease, says Woodwell, would reduce the global "carbon budget" of the atmosphere by two and a half billion tons, almost enough to eliminate the three-billion-ton annual increase. Measures to reduce deforestation could make up the additional half a billion tons, he says.

Such goals, he insists, are reachable, in part through tighter conservation measures. "Our initial analyses suggest that a 50 percent reduction is possible [in the industrial world] without changing GNP [gross national product] very much. We're already doing things with cars and houses that have reduced the use of energy by fifty percent, and we can do much, much more."

The developing world, however, presents a more serious challenge. In Third World countries, says Ted Gordon, "fossil fuel burning is the principal source of energy, and to engage in goals that limit fossil fuel burning worldwide deprives most people in the world of their source of heat."

To be sure, there are some positive factors. The developing nations tend to lie in the low latitudes, where more solar energy is available. And even within current patterns of energy use there is a potential for conservation, a point emphasized by Patrick Mungai.

"The question is not whether there is enough energy," says Mungai. "The question is, How efficiently are we using the natural resources that are available?" If the average family in Kenya burns a ton of wood over a certain period of time, he says, "the question is, How can you make them use that ton of wood more effectively?"

డ

Finding ways to do better with less has long been a goal of Vineet Narain. Now a staff reporter with *Jansatta,* the leading Hindu daily in India, he has been involved in what he calls "rural activism" for the last decade, making television documentaries on rural life, and helping bring some one hundred and fifty foreign students to Indian villages for extended stays. A tall young man with a broad mustache and a thirst for thoughtful conversation, he stands at a cultural crossroads where old-world standards of manners and hospitality (he brought Indian-made gifts to his hosts at our conference) blend with 21st century concerns for global interdependence and the dignity of the oppressed.

Clearly engaged by the scientific discussion of environmental issues, he comes to it from another perspective. "Mohandas Gandhi, many years ago, talked of environmental protection in a very different way, as a question of individual attitude," he says. "What is our attitude towards nature? Are we all the time drawing resources from nature, consuming them, and throwing them away; or are we repaying anything to nature? Do we owe something to nature?"

"So much is wasted in this society," he observes. Case in point: the production of solid wastes. Every time he flies to the West and has a meal on an international flight, he finds that "20 percent of it is edible, and the rest is all garbage: so many colorful packing materials, so much tissue paper."

As an example of an alternative, he notes that "in India recently people have developed something like your paper plates: They take the big leaves of trees, press them in a kind of mold, and make a dried plate for parties." Unlike a paper plate, however, it costs no trees to produce. And after the party, when the plate is thrown away, it naturally decays and "recirculates into nature."

Such local solutions to local problems hold promise, he feels, while those brought in from developed nations sometimes fail. In many Indian villages, he notes, "we can do without a flush system" for toilets. Yet flush systems are "exactly what's happening in India. We have no drinking water in [many] villages, but we have a flush system which is polluting so much of the water."

The issue, then, is one of appropriate technology, suited to the conditions of the society in which it is applied. A much-used term, it's one that Gordon distrusts. "Appropriate technology is a very glib, let's-make-it-smaller-because-it's-got-to-be-better stereotype," he says. "It may well be that large-scale technology is quite appropriate for some of these problems."

Not everyone agrees. "I find it puzzling," interjects Tommy Odemwingie, "that anybody could be distrustful of appropriate technology." The industrial nations, he admits, have all sorts of fine technologies. In the developing world, however, "we cannot afford the technology that exists in the developed countries."

"The reason I distrust appropriate technologies," Gordon rejoins, "is because it's come to mean in many people's minds simple things that can be put together simply: a solar pump, a steam hoe." In the near future, however, "high technology prices will drop, and high technology may well be appropriate to solve some of the problems that are most onerous and pressing in the Third World. A high-technology solar cell, for example: The price may really drop, and it may be really a very good source of energy and very appropriate for use throughout the world.

"I don't want to take developed country technology and throw it pell-mell into the Third World," he insists. "I think that's wrong. But there certainly is a class of technology which is not simple, which may today be at the frontier, and which may be really quite appropriate to use in Third World countries to solve specific problems."

Odemwingie brings the discussion back to the education of those using the technology. He points out that if the technology is not understood, the result will be a deepening dependence on the West. The sort of technology he finds helpful, he says, must work in "a situation where people don't even know how to read or write."

As an editor, he points out, "I have had the privilege of using features from a feature service based in Nairobi, partly supported by the United Nations Environment Program. It tries to relate to the people at the village level how they can [use] an idea without unduly destroying the environment, and the techniques are simple and therefore appropriate. That is what we understand by the old concept of appropriate technology."

For Michael Hooker, both these arguments make sense. "As I understand appropriate technology, I'm wholly in favor of it," he says. "And I also agree with Ted [Gordon] that most people who use that locution don't have the faintest idea what they are talking about, and it becomes a dangerous buzz word.

"I worry," he continues, "about the alienation that will come in the future, when we are a thoroughly technology-infused society and most of us don't have the darnedest idea how computers work." His answer: some form of technological education in both developed and developing nations.

"I think that speaks to Vineet Narain's point about our relationship to our environment," he explains, "in that if we understand how technology works, how the carbon cycle functions, how photosynthesis works, how we've overtaxed the capacity of the earth to perform photosynthesis to keep an ecobalance—if we understand that, if we grow up as children understanding that, then we might develop a certain reverence for the environment as a system in balance."

Moreover, Hooker feels that technology holds all kinds of answers for environmental issues. "I think protein engineering is going to take care of the world's food problem. It's going to take care of the energy problem. It's going to take care of the photosynthesis problem. And I think it's going to happen much sooner than any of us realize."

Promising as such technologies may be, the immediate problem for developing nations, say many observers, focuses on a single issue: better redistribution of current assets. Such redistribution, in an increasingly interdependent world, may

59

require new methods of accounting. "What we need," says Clark, "is a set of *environmental* accounts that take seriously the notion that resources and environment are part of the productive stock of a society, just the way that the capital-stock investment in a factory or an educational system is part of the productive future potential of that area."

That, however, is not happening. At present, says Clark, international accounting is structured so that "in virtually every country of the world you actually get credits into your national accounts by chopping down a forest and washing the soil into a river; it's a positive benefit in your gross domestic product."

As serious as these are, the problems facing the environment go beyond the distinctions between the developed and the developing world. Much of the overload on the environment can be traced to what many regard as an excessive growth of human population: currently five billion, and heading for between nine and fourteen billion in the next century.

Humans, according to Peter Raven, author of one of the papers commissioned for the conference, share their environment with at least five million other species of plant and animal life.* One way to measure human dominance, writes Raven, "is to calculate the proportion of the total energy available [on earth each year] that we appropriate for ourselves: What fraction of the total do [humans] consume directly, waste, or co-opt (as in clearing pastures)?"

The answer, he reports, is about 40 percent—a figure that is steadily rising as human population increases. "If we achieve no improvements in the ways in which we use the

* Dr. Raven was unable to attend the conference at the last moment for personal reasons. His paper, however, was instrumental in guiding our discussions, and is reprinted in shortened form in the Appendix.

world's resources," he warns, "we would need 80 percent of the total by the middle of the next century just to stay even."

Just as one can apportion the use of energy between human and non-human forms of life, so, in the human community, one can apportion the use of resources between developed and developing nations. And there, reports Raven, the contrast is even more stark. "The use of industrial energy or minerals by the industrialized world amounts to 90 percent of the total available [worldwide] for most commodities," he writes.

All of which brings Hooker back around to the one thing that most needs to change: attitudes. "I'm concerned mostly," he says, "about Vineet's point, about the obscene avariciousness with which we consume resources." That fact, he says, "tells me that there's something wrong spiritually with us; that we, at least in American society, consume material culture, use it up, spend it, waste it." As a result, he feels, we "pollute the environment in a blind fashion that takes the place of what would otherwise be the metaphysical substance of our lives, which is missing."

ತಿ

That's a point Shirley Williams has spent much of her political career trying to make. After serving as Secretary of Education and Science in the last Labour government, Mrs. Williams left the party to help found the Social Democratic Party. A devoted Europeanist, she is currently Joint President of the still newer Social and Liberal Democrats.

Even among those who find her left-of-center views anathema, Williams remains one of the much-liked figures in British politics. She is known for addressing problems with a forthrightness and affection more often found in a chat across a garden fence than in a speech on the hustings, a point to which this reporter can personally attest. A decade ago, I first met her during a break in a conference at a country estate outside London where, needing to get several hundred letters into the next mail for her constituents, she agreed to an interview but found she couldn't lick stamps and talk at the same time. Her solution was characteristically practical. "You lick," she said as we sat on a sofa in the entrance hall, "and I'll talk."

That practicality is evident in her approach to environmental issues, about which she cares deeply. Among her suggestions:

- All private-sector firms should be required to make public statements about "their use and return of the resources of the world outside, the balance of inputs and outputs in terms of finite reserves of environmental resources in the world as a whole." Simply translated, that means that they would have to "go out and plant trees if they've cut trees down; and one could see that as part of the accounting system of firms." The goal, she says, is to have firms be responsible "over a time period to replace what they take out."

- The World Bank, the International Monetary Fund, and the industrial nations should agree to "pay rent" to the developing nations in order to help preserve vital environmental resources. "If we're all going to be destroyed by the warming of the world, and at the same time we are putting the most immense pressure on the Brazils and the Argentinas to produce more cash crops in order to pay the interest on their debts, that means they cut down the forests to plant coffee. And after five years the land is sterile because the soil can't sustain coffee for very long." Insofar as that is happening, she says, "we in the

West have to answer for the fact that we are speeding up the destruction of the environment on which we ourselves depend." The only way to stop that process is "for the West to accept its commitment to the sustaining of the environment on an international basis."

• Given that fossil-fuel use is one of the primary problems, she says that the rest of the world should "be leaning on the American government like mad to raise energy taxes. It is ludicrous that energy is priced where it is in the United States today, absolutely ludicrous. The United States ought at the very minimum to bring itself in line with the rest of the Western industrialized world as far as imported energy is concerned."

Williams also feels that the Western world in general "ought to adopt a regime of steadily increasing energy prices, a common regime to get away from the competitivity problems." Under such a system, any fall in oil prices would be offset by "a sustained steady increase in price," in order to stimulate energy conservation.

Gordon agrees. Most energy research and development (R&D) programs, he says, are "tied to the price of petroleum. When the price of oil is high, R&D is high. R&D is engaged in because of the promise of future profit, and when the promise of future profit is low because the prices of fuel are low, we have no incentive to do the R&D. There ought to be another mechanism in place that encourages R&D independent of the price of oil."

How to establish such mechanisms? That's long been one of Robert McNamara's concerns. Despite increasing global interdependence, coupled with an increasing recognition that environmental problems transcend national boundaries, the former World Bank president worries that most

63

environmental decisions are still made by individual nations. "We do not have institutional forums appropriate to this increasingly interdependent world," he says, adding that the United Nations Environment Program, if strengthened, could become such a forum.

Needed beyond that, however, is "an organized international effort to reverse the present trend of environmental degradation." McNamara worries that "there is no recognition today of what's happening. I'm just scared to death of what's happening in Africa. The forests are being cut down, the land is eroding, the water's mismanaged; and it's occurring at a pace that is going to lead to results within ten to twenty years that are horrible."

The problem, he says, is that, rather than take action, some parts of the public-policy community prefer to do more studies, insisting that not enough is yet known to act. McNamara cites President Reagan's dealings with Canada on the acid rain issue, an example of delaying action because there was no definitive proof of a cause-and-effect relationship.

"I agree," says McNamara, "You can't prove it." He worries, however, that the issue resembles the debate over the health hazards of tobacco. For twenty years, he says, the nation argued about whether tobacco smoke caused disease. Today, he says, "I'm not absolutely certain, but the probabilities are that it does. And since a lot of people are going to die if we don't say that, we ought to say it."

That leads him to his central point: that "you're not going to have the certainty of causal relationships on these matters that are potentially irreversible to our environment." His three-fold solution:

- "Buy insurance" by taking action, since the risks of doing nothing outweigh the dangers of mistaking the proper remedy.

- "Negotiate deals" through the appropriate forums, making the tradeoffs necessary to save the environment.

- "Stimulate at every level—the individual level, the firm level, the national level, the international level—more sensitivity" to environmental issues.

A call for further research, however, is not always a means of delaying action, a point he illustrates by citing the African population problem, a driving force behind environmental degradation. The World Bank, he says, developed programs to reduce the fertility rate in Kenya, in 1972 and again in 1979. "The last time I was there, about five or seven years ago," he recalls, [President Daniel arap] Moi said to me, 'This is [still] my number one problem.' What's happened? The fertility rate has *increased*. Today it's eight point zero, which means the average female in reproductive years produces eight children."

And that, he says, is "a disaster. The question is what to do about it. I don't know. There isn't anybody around this table, if you were given absolute authority to go to Kenya today to do what was needed to reduce that fertility, nobody knows." In this case, he says, the need is for "more research" into the "appropriate technology" for that region and culture.

What comes through McNamara's words is the sense of urgency about the problem, a feeling shared by those around the table: humanity no longer has the luxury of waiting until the causes of environmental degradation are wholly understood. "If you wait until causality is established," quips Harvard University sociologist Amitai Etzioni, "we will be dead, environmentally and otherwise."

If Etzioni hadn't said that, former Colorado governor Richard Lamm might have. A tall man with a shock of prematurely white hair, a wide smile, and the smooth grace of a ready conversationalist, his appearance belies both his old nickname, "Governor Gloom," and the depth of thought that informs his concern for the world. After fellow Coloradan John Naisbitt wrote his buoyantly optimistic book, *Megatrends: Ten New Directions Transforming Our Lives,* Governor Lamm countered with his far less sanguine *Megatraumas: America at the Year 2000.* A bundle of energy, Lamm told me just before leaving the governorship in 1987 that the year-long appointment he'd accepted at Dartmouth College was designed to give him a chance to "rewire down from two-twenty to one-ten" volts.

The rewiring hasn't hurt his ebullience. Explaining, in mock seriousness, that he has found "the root cause" of mankind's environmental problem, he refers the Wingspread group to author Loren C. Eiseley's description of early primates. "Eisley said there were two bands of apes back in the early millennia," he explains. "One of them was a very honest and kind band of apes, who were faithful to their wives and were clean and bathed and lived without being wasteful. The other were dirty and dishonest, unfaithful to their wives, and wasted their resources: an awful band of apes.

"One of these bands discovered fire and became our ancestors. Guess which one?"

The anecdote draws chuckles. But the jest raises a profound ontological issue: What is the nature of man, and what is man's inherent relation to his environment? Is he willfully destructive of his surroundings, or only ignorantly so? Must he be pushed by the force of law into husbanding resources, or can he be drawn toward higher goals through reasoned instruction? Or, as our moderator, Adam Yarmolinsky, reformulates the question, What is the balance between "the kicks and the carrots" that can stimulate action?

For Shirley Williams, the answer lies in a balance. "We're producing a whole series of lovely goals," she notes, referring to the conference agenda. But as a politician, she says, "I'd look to them and just shrug my shoulders and say, 'Well, fine, I agree. But none of them is going to happen.'

"We've got to consider," she adds, "how we build up enough momentum to make them actually begin to happen. If we have nothing but list after list of desirable ends, none of them will happen. I think we've got to get on to the nitty gritty of actually looking at the forums, looking at the pressures, looking at how we make [these goals] grip on governments."

For Lamm, that's eminently practical wisdom. Environmental problems, he says, are "so hard to quantify when you're sitting there trying to decide the relative risk." He notes that, as governor, he had to spend forty million dollars cleaning up "mill tailings that are going to cause one cancer death maybe every ten years."

"Now, you give me that forty million dollars to stop smoking or deal with toxic and hazardous waste," he adds, and it might well produce a far greater impact. Then why go after mill tailings? Because, he says, it's a fairly straightforward and measurable problem, unlike many more important environmental issues that don't lend themselves to easy quantification.

It reminds him, he concludes, of "looking for your keys under the lamppost (even though that isn't where you lost them) because that's where the light is. We protect ourselves over here because that's where the program is—many times missing, over there, lots more hazardous environmental risks because we don't quantify them."

But quantification itself, for Matina Horner, isn't enough. "Assuming we did get the data and knew exactly what the issues were so we could formulate the priorities and make a convincing case for what they might be," she says, "I'm still struggling with how we confront and resolve the enormous conflicts that are generated both within and between the individual, local, regional, and global arenas.

"There will clearly be enormous conflicts about whose rights and whose responsibilities are going to be put in," she adds. Needed is "an interdependent arena to redefine rights and responsibilities and the appropriate balance between them."

As an example, she cites her home state of Massachusetts. While it may be true that "there's more than enough energy already in the United States," there seems not to be enough in Massachusetts to carry an expanding state economy to its next stage. And that's not a problem Massachusetts alone can resolve, since a solution in Massachusetts's favor might leave other energy-poor states groping for what they regard as their fair share.

Or take the case for land-use plans on a national rather than local or regional scale. In many nations, says Woodwell, "a national land-use plan seems to me to be essential because decisions about land use are all relegated to the smallest political bodies least able to manage those decisions. No one is thinking about how many square miles it takes to produce water for New York City, how much forest it takes to keep that water clean, how much forest there ought to be in North America to stabilize resources that North America needs, and other such issues." Nor is anyone willing to face the sacrifices required to make such plans work.

And if that's a problem on a national scale, what happens

internationally? "Who is going to decide," asks Horner, "that they should make the sacrifice for the global arena, and how do we go about educating and helping people do that? I must say I am totally puzzled about who's going to give up their rights or see that it's their responsibility to hold back in order that someplace else will benefit."

That very issue of give-and-take, says Clark, is "the central problem." While acknowledging that humanity needs more scientific knowledge, he sees the real problem as "this absence of forums and mechanisms" of the sort that concern Horner.

He remains encouraged, however, by the small-scale models currently working. "We're already having some success with establishing for a small region a watershed or airshed that decides, usually somewhat arbitrarily, that the system can withstand this much input of pollution." The next step, he adds, is to start parceling out—"sometimes by selling pollutant rights, sometimes by straight legislative fiat"— the amount of pollution that different firms and users are permitted to add to the system. He cites the Montreal Protocol for the protection of the ozone layer, signed in 1987 by twenty-four nations and designed to limit the production of chlorofluorocarbons (CFCs), as an example of a workable model.

"I think we have to begin codifying our experience with [these models], saying what types of environment development trade-offs do we have experience with," he concludes.

One thing seems clear: Developing models, however difficult, may bring rewards that stretch beyond environmental issues. No one thinks the process will be easy, given the global, intergenerational, financial, scientific, and ethical ramifications of many environmental issues. But Los Angeles attorney and community activist Joan Abrahamson spoke for us all when she identified, in the global overcast, something

69

not unlike a silver lining. "Maybe," she said, "the identification of the common threat to the world through the environment is another way to unify us, as sad as that is. Maybe by developing appropriate technology to combat this threat, we can learn how to do cooperative problem solving that might even be related to security issues and other issues that face us."

Chapter 5

Ethics

Theodore J. Gordon has the one essential credential of a futurist: He's interested in just about everything.

Founder of a private consulting firm that helps clients navigate in the face of future uncertainties, he's overseen studies on everything from the future of copper tubing use in the air-conditioning industry to the question of American policy toward the Caribbean region in the year 2000. As his firm, The Futures Group, has grown from small beginnings in 1971 to a multimillion-dollar operation with a professional staff of seventy-five, so his own insight into 21st century concerns has expanded. Trained as an aerospace engineer (he spent sixteen years with McDonnell Douglas, where he was chief engineer for the Saturn program), he now moves easily from what he calls his "specialty" areas in technology and scientific research to the broader ranges of social, philosophical, and moral issues facing mankind's future.

Energetic, direct, and good-humored, Gordon wastes little time getting to the core of an issue. As our discussion turned to ethics — the kinds of choices people make in what they pursue and how they pursue it — he phrased the central question in two words: "What matters?"

For Gordon, the answer entails setting priorities and focusing on issues of greatest import. But which are they? In what he admits is only "a partial attempt to answer the question about what matters," he identifies five elements that go into making the right choice.

"What matters are those things which are irreversible, those issues which put us into the situation of making decisions that cannot be backed out of easily. What matters are those things that are immediate: Immediate problems are more important than those that are in the distant future. What matters are those problems that affect many people as opposed to few people. What matters are those issues that are severe in their effects. And what matters are those issues for which there are responses: I would rather tackle an issue for which there is some chance of action than an issue for which there seems to be no approach."

That his analysis grows out of a moral imperative—a need for better processes for making choices—is clear. Clear, too, is the relevance of Gordon's categories in assessing the state of global morality. Asked to identify the leading "what matters" issue for the late twentieth century, more than a few people point to the breakdown of public and private morality. Greed, selfishness, dishonesty, lack of trust, infidelity, corruption—those sorts of issues, in the eyes of many, fit squarely into Gordon's five categories. They have immediate impact, widespread distribution, and severe consequences. They are addressable, as the increasing interest in upgrading the ethics of business, sports, academics, politics, the media, the family, and religious life attests. Finally, there is growing agreement that, left unaddressed, the effects may prove irreversible. It may well be, as Russian poet Andrei Voznesensky says, that "the 21st century will not *be*" unless morality becomes part of what he calls our "practical, pragmatic, day-by-day things."

But can morality be pragmatic? In some ways, it already is. "Most people," says Robert McNamara, "are basically moral." Yet paradoxically, he adds, "we don't bring to a consideration of public-policy issues a moral foundation. My experience in public-policy debates has been that you're thought to be rather naive if you introduce the moral dimension."

It is this paradox—the contradiction between the morality of private individuals and the amoral stance of public institutions—that, for many observers, characterizes the late twentieth century. Even the churches, says McNamara, often "stay away" from moral issues. "I received a medal for ten years' attendance at Sunday School in the 1920s," he recalls. "I never once in ten years heard the issue of racial discrimination discussed in the church." He notes that "in our society the churches, Protestant and Catholic, failed to deal with that issue for roughly a century."

For McNamara, that refusal consitutes a moral failure. By moral, he means "an understanding that our behavior—our national [and] our individual behavior—does affect other people, and that we have a responsibility to behave in a manner consistent with the basic rights of others.

"By the end of the century we should seek to increase awareness of and sensitivity to the moral dimensions of the behavior both of individuals and nations," he says. "In particular, we should stress the immorality of the United States and the Soviet Union and their allies unilaterally adopting security strategies that place at risk the survival of other nations. We should stress the immorality of the rich consuming a disproportionate share of limited resources, with adverse effects on other individuals and future generations and other nations. And we should stress the immorality of contributing to the degradation of the environment, again with adverse effects on other individuals and other nations and future generations.

"There is a moral dimension to each of these major subjects we've been discussing," he concludes, "but very rarely do you see in public debate a discussion of the morality of them."

ॐ

Making morality practical, however, requires a commitment by individuals. That depends on individual choice. Yet some of the severest cricitism leveled at late-twentieth-century ethics revolves around the issue of excessive individualism, a point raised by attorney Kathleen Kennedy Townsend.

Argumentative but not belligerent, persistent but not rude, Townsend brings a formidable vitality and a great warmth to discussions of global issues. She currently works for the Department of Education in Maryland, overseeing a program to involve young people in community service. She sees community service as "a way to build character," which she feels addresses "one of the major issues" facing the United States. "I think it's very important that young people have a sense of responsibility," she adds. Some four years ago, she helped found the Robert Kennedy Human Rights Award in honor of her father, Robert F. Kennedy.

She is troubled, however, by a tendency among those who think about ethics, "especially left-wing intellectuals who are usually interested in the kind of issues that we've raised," to refuse to consider ethics in a religious context. They are typically uncomfortable, she finds, with "talking about God and morality. And I find this very unfortunate, because so many people across the world care very deeply about God and religion."

She says she is still "trying to digest" a discussion she recently had while working among black elementary-school students in Baltimore who had been targeted as potential dropouts. Since most came from one-parent homes or were in foster care, they were in a church basement one day for after-school day care.

"I asked the minister, 'Do you ever talk about God to these children?' And the minister's reaction was, 'No, why should we talk about God? What would God have to say to these young people? That means nothing.' "

She feels strongly, on the contrary, that those in leadership roles in America need to help "make it more possible to talk about God," and particularly about the relation of religion to the nation's ethical traditions. "These are not just republican traditions, not just the sectarian traditions," she says, noting that many of our values "really do come from a belief in God."

One aspect of these ethical traditions that especially concerns Townsend is the balance of individual rights and community responsibilities. "We live in a country that promotes individual achievement, individual success, and that breeds economic success as well," she says. "And we've become the richest nation in the world, in large part because of our ideal of the individual.

"At the same time, once you touch that kind of success, that sort of richness, it's hard to go back to create the republican virtues of truth and honesty and fellow-feeling for other individuals, and a sense of responsibility not only for yourself but for how other people live."

One way to recover those virtues, she feels, lies in "the idea of getting young people involved in a youth corps or in some sort of service to their community, as a way to reinstill those republican virtues that are important not only for the United States to *survive* but also for the United States to *take responsibility.*"

Townsend notes that it has become popular to blame individualism for present-day "excesses of selfishness." But she adds that "there are great things about individual liberty, and the ability to write and to think what you want."

Amitai Etzioni, agreeing, brings these two poles together.

"We need to recognize that both the society and the individual are essential to a morality which we can use in the next century," he says.

"Marx, from my viewpoint, was as wrong as you can be," he continues, except in pointing out that "you have to argue inside history and not outside of history." The history of a culture, Etzioni notes, determines its position along the scale that runs from collectivism to individualism. "I think China and the Soviet Union, who have been erring [by] being excessively collectivistic, are now discovering the beauty of the individual. But I think that the Anglo-Saxon societies are discovering the need for a commons. There's suddenly new talk about the affirmative role of the community.

"Obviously the light lies in some kind of balancing between individual rights and the need for a commons, between obligations and entitlements," he says. "If we could enter the next century with a wider recognition of that balance, and get away from either collectivistic excesses or the celebration of radical individualism, I think we'd be better for it."

For Matina Horner, this balance results in a kind of collective activity of individuals that she refers to as *trusteeship.* "The morality that we're talking about," she says, consists of "learning somehow how to exercise our role and responsibilities as trustees of the human and natural resources of the world community in which we live.

"What is it," she asks, "that we invest in—be it health, education, welfare, aid policies—and what is it that we *refrain* from investing in? And why and how do we execute this [trustees'] role?" Noting that "mutual trusteeship" may be "a better word than *morality,"* she asks, "What are the ties that bring us together as trustees?"

One essential set of ties, she argues, are those that produce what she calls "intergenerational bonding," or the ties that create a sense of trusteeship among generations. On that point, Richard Lamm expresses real concern that the balance of power among the generations has become skewed. "One of the dilemmas that I've spent the last few months thinking about," he says, "is the power of the senior lobby," a force he describes as "the 800-pound gorilla in American politics."

The elderly, he observes, make up 12 percent of the U.S. population. Yet they get 56 percent of the nation's entitlements, such as Social Security and Medicare. "We have the highest life expectancy at the age of eighty of any country in the world," he continues, "and yet we have one of the highest infant mortality rates in the industrialized world."

As a former office-holder, he notes that "when the elderly lobby talks, you listen. There are almost as many members of the AARP [American Association of Retired Persons] as there are in the Republican Party." There is, however, no equivalent lobby representing children—not a surprising fact, since children don't vote. The result, he feels, is that "money desperately needed to educate our kids, or for health care or vaccination for kids, is being sent to senior citizens."

Given the fact that "allocation of resources in the United States is really governed by special interests and by whoever pushes hardest against the system," Lamm notes that "the quality of life of tomorrow is going to suffer very significantly because one cohort in our demography is pushing so hard and so effectively to gather so many resources at the expense of a very significant number of [young] people."

And that, for Lamm, constitutes a moral issue. "I think that there has to be some recognition on the part of the elderly lobby that there are other generations involved." He worries about "the sense of entitlement" on the part of some senior citizens, who feel they have *earned* all they receive in government subsidies. For the sake of clarity, he says, "we ought to divide every social security check into two parts.

Number one says, 'This is what you get back because of what you invested.' It would be one seventh of the check." The other six sevenths, he says, would be labeled "'welfare from your children'": money paid to support the elderly by those still working.

The attention paid to children, in fact, is widely seen as central to any set of ethical goals for the coming century. "One of the moral considerations that unites us all, whether we're a developed nation or a developing nation," says Michael Hooker, "is our children.

"The century that we're talking about preparing for is really the century of our children, not of ourselves," he adds. The goal of any future-oriented thinking, then, is "preparing our children for the 21st century, and thereby preparing the 21st century for civilization."

How to do that? "I have in mind something analagous to a child's bill of rights," Hooker explains. "The bill of rights would be both generic and specific—specific to the condition of children in various parts of the world. In developing nations, it may pertain to nutrition, to child labor laws, to child servitude, and so forth. In all nations it would pertain to education, and in the developed nations especially there should be a very strong element of transcultural education."

Inherent in such transcultural education would be an awareness of living conditions in less fortunate nations, a kind of moral awareness that should help prompt action. "In our part of the world," says Olusegun Obasanjo, the quality of life appears to be determined by "the amount of degradation, starvation, erosion of land, deterioration in agricultural production, and the uncertainty of rainfall." Yet crucial to the quality of life is the ethical dimension. "Is there a way," he asks, "by which values, morality, can make within our nations [a sense of] sharing and caring?"

The solution, he says, lies in educating all the world's

children—not only those in the developed nations—to be leaders of the 21st century. "What sort of morality are we going to inculcate in them? Are they going to feel that they have responsibility only for their immediate environment, their immediate community? Or are they going to have a sense of mankind [that will] make them feel that what happens elsewhere in the universe affects them?"

Transcultural education, however, is not limited to educating children. Adults, too, need to be educated about the developing world, a point made in heartfelt terms by Kristin Helmore.

"I think the media has a tremendous potential in the field of education of the public," she says. "Very often the only verbal or pictorial images of Africa in the [news media] are of starving children in Ethiopia, for example. One thing the media can be encouraged to do is to portray the Third World not without its problems, but with its dignity intact, to portray as much of a sense of dynamism and resourcefulness and self-reliance as you portray a sense of problems, because that is the reality.

"There are plenty of people in the developing world tackling their problems," she adds, "yet the image that is presented to the developed world very often is only one of need and disaster. I believe people would care more, would want to help more, would be able to identify more, if they were allowed to respect the peoples in developing countries more. I think that people don't want to help each other when they feel they're distanced and when they are not able to put themselves in each other's positions.

"I think we are all exactly the same," she concludes, "and the only difference is our context. If people can put themselves in another person's position, they will be more concerned about looking for ways that they can help."

In any conference there are those who listen with the head. They seem to be all ears, all rationality, all articulation. They have several postures: a forward lean, as though to clamber right onto the table, or a backward tilt, seeking an Olympian detachment in which to contemplate the currents of thought. Fastening almost visibly onto ideas, they either tune out entirely—so captivated that they launch off onto their own silent lines of arguments—or become so exercised that they can hardly wait for an opportunity to reply. Of such are lively conferences made.

But there are also those who listen with the heart. Theirs is a middle posture—upright, peaceful, still. What matters to them is not so much the expression of ideas, although they listen carefully to the ebb and flow of the dialogue, as the impressions made by the attitudes behind the words. They think, one might say, feelingly. They seem to be nourished less by their own or others' individual words than by the sensitivities distilled from entire conversations. Of such are meaningful conferences made.

Stella Maria is of the latter group. Although she heads the Institute for Women within the All Indonesian Workers Union, she hardly fits the image of a trade unionist. Polite, demure, quiet almost to the point of reticence, she speaks softly and thoughtfully, ending her rare interventions by thanking her audience for listening.

So she would never have dreamed of interrupting Obasanjo. If she had, however, she might have put forth the mirror image of one of his ideas. He noted the need for students in the developing world to understand that "what happens elsewhere in the universe affects them." Maria sees an equally powerful need for the obverse: to have them understand that what they themselves do can affect the universe. "My basic concern," she explains, "is how to get the female —which is half of the population of Indonesia—to be conscious that they have a potential input and effect on the international society, that they can participate and have self-confidence."

Like Obasanjo, she too is engaged by the "quality of life" issues. For her, however, the term includes far more than material benefits. She clarifies the point by citing an example. In the Indonesian villages, she explains, most people "haven't got anything" of a material nature. So a trial program was recently established to bring some of the very poorest villagers into the city, where they were given good accommodations and jobs as domestics.

The result? "I find after reading their diaries (there were a hundred diaries) that they felt much happier in their poor village than in the city, because the values and the perceptions are totally different," she says. Her conclusion: Social needs that may appear to be universal are in fact "different for different cultures and social levels of people.

"When you talk about quality of life and environmental issues," she says, "I think for our countries it's totally different. Maybe we can find certain points and items where we do agree, but to achieve quality of life, I think you should take into consideration the culture of the country and the economic situation."

One aspect of culture that needs to be considered is the level of education, a point she feels is sometimes overlooked by Westerners intent on providing help. At this time, the immediate need in Indonesia is simply for basic schooling. "In my country," she notes, "there is not yet compulsory formal education for the total population."

Yet if for Maria a central issue is the lack of education, for others it is the quality of whatever education is already being delivered. "I think too often we confuse information with knowledge and technical expertise with wisdom," says

Nazir Ahmad. "I think a lot of the time we talk about skills instead of trying to develop a perspective."

"I'm reminded," he adds, "of what Chairman Mao talked about in terms of education in most of the Third World, that it mostly trains the memory and confines the mind." Instead, Ahmad sees education as having several goals. First, it "allows an individual to map herself or himself within the environment where she or he is, to get people very early on to think of themselves in the context of the larger world.

"Second, I think education needs to introduce the notion of choice. You cannot have everything you want. There are choices and trade-offs that you have to make. But a lot of the time, especially in the Third World, education is just thrust upon you: You are on one trajectory or another, depending on where you were born and all the other things that happen.

"The introduction of choice allows, obviously, for consideration of a wider range of possibilities. And it can be a very empowering thing, especially for younger people as they're growing up.

"Third, consistent both with the religious kinds of things that Kathleen [Townsend] was talking about and with the moral climate of really understanding the individual and society as inseparable, I think that in every culture, whether in its folklore or its cultural traditions or its religious traditions, you find a lot of support for [the teaching of] certain irreducible rights and responsibilities."

That kind of moral education, he says, far from being "culture specific," includes some broad elements. "The rights of children is a beginning of it," he says. But it also includes such things as leadership training, using "a cooperative learning environment where people both have to follow as well as take initiative," as well as "a healthy skepticism, if you will, for both laws and authority."

The latter he sees as especially important, particularly for the developing world, where legal structures may be fragile and the rule of law not deeply rooted. The need, he says, is "to create an environment in which authority is not just taken for granted," but where, instead, it is reexamined "on a continuous basis." For future generations, he says, that reexamination "is going to be really important" if the developing nations are to continue "embracing the possibility of change."

Mention *change* in the context of *education*, and most conversations shift almost immediately into discussions of technology. Granted, the developing nations generally recognize their need for technological education, a point made by Nigerian journalist Tommy Odemwingie, who insists that education must provide at least a rudimentary understanding of technology. Yet too often in the developing world, he says, the attempt is made to apply "a very advanced technology in a situation stuck in illiteracy. In the final analysis the people for whom technology is supposed to solve the problem don't even understand the technology."

Not surprisingly, then, the components of education that both Nazir Ahmad and Maria call for have little to do with technology. And that, according to Shuichi Kato, may not simply be an oversight. As we move into the next century, he says, "the major question is not how to *develop* technology but how to *use* technology."

Not denying the importance of technology, Kato wants to see it kept in its proper historical perspective. "Every generation," he says, "is conditioned by the culture of the age." The twentieth century, he adds, is "characterized by the technological culture, first, and also perhaps by [the prominence of] powerful organizations." Not surprisingly, the efforts to resolve some of the major problems facing the twentieth century—East-West relations, North-South relations, environmental issues, education—have been dominated by the "consequences of our culture, which was a technological culture and overwhelmed by organization."

If these efforts, growing out of modern culture, have essentially failed (and Kato believes they have), then what will future efforts bring? That will depend on the direction of future culture. And what will characterize that culture?

Immersed in our own culture, says Kato, we have difficulty seeing into the future, just as, a century ago, our ancestors had difficulty imagining transportation systems based on flight or musical compositions building on Stravinsky. Yet even without knowing the shape of the future, says Kato, "we might somehow help prepare the next generation through education, not only the school education but also the social education."

At present, there are two sorts of education. One, he says, teaches "how to build the laboratory of Solomon's kingdom," while the other teaches "how to appreciate, really seriously, the beauty of the small flowers." Today's schooling features an "overwhelmingly strong emphasis on scientific and technological education." The education of the future, he says, needs something else. "I don't know what is the 'something else,'" he adds. "You might call it humanities, but I would call it poetry or arts."

Such an education would clearly focus on moral principles. "Science, technology, the desire for power, how to control the nations: all this derives from the culture which is based on building up Solomon's kingdom's laboratory," he says. "But perhaps education should be switched over to [a different] emphasis, not ignoring the first one, the knowledge of science technology, but shifted to put the stress on a certain mental, poetical ability to appreciate seriously the lilies in the field."

And that's just the sort of appreciation that Katharine Whitehorn understands. She and I first met several years ago at Ditchley, an august estate in Oxfordshire which, like Wingspread, plays host to international conferences. Having newspapering in common, we spent part of a drizzling February afternoon traipsing around the sprawling grounds, pausing now and then in our conversation to absorb the muted, liquid beauty of the English winter.

An engaging writer whose widely read columns appear in the London Sunday *Observer,* Whitehorn insists that "I write only in a general way and have no speciality." Her writing and conversation, however, reveal her as a clear-eyed moralist in the best sense of that word. Firmly grounded in family life (she and her husband, novelist Gavin Lyall, have raised two children and managed two careers with utmost grace) she grasps and articulates the value of marriage in an age greatly troubled by that institution. Deeply concerned by what she sees as some of the excesses, uncaring attitudes, and shortsighted measures of modern governments, she is nevertheless no mere anti-establishment liberal: She sits on the board of directors of a British savings and loan institution, where she says she is "well placed to see the mechanisms of human selfishness." Involved with the Royal Society of Medicine in London, she serves on a working party of the World Health Organization dealing with issues of mental health.

Not surprisingly, then, her concerns are pragmatic ones involving how to bring ethical ideas to bear on the world's daily life. That means, for her, that these ideas need to be made applicable to "the only global culture we actually have, which is the commercial culture, the man in the blue suit."

"If we want to get more conception of morality into the 21st century," she says, "we've somehow got to make businessmen feel that they gain some clout from moral behavior, not only on Sundays but in their business. We've got to get them away from the idea that we must do *well* before we can do *good,* and revive some conception of a business ethic.

"I think that most people work for the approval of their fellows," she continues. "If the only way you're going to get approval from the community in which you work is because your multinational has taken over two other multinationals and nobody particularly notices what you've done to the environment or the community, that's what these men are going to go for."

Changing such behavior requires changing the structure of approval. Whenever this "commercial culture" acts in ways that contribute to global progress, she says, "you need to praise, to reward, to show these people that they have done something that will make them feel good."

"I think it's the responsibility of business leaders to be sensitive to the public good," says McNamara. Recalling his experience at the Ford Motor Company, he notes that "the auto industry had to be pulled screaming and hollering into safety, environment, and energy conservation. The auto industry should have *led* in addressing [those] problems."

Would taking the lead in such ethical issues have jeopardized bottom-line considerations? "I could take any one of those three [problems] and make a profit on it," says McNamara. "You can merchandise safety. You can merchandise emission controls. You can merchandise energy conservation."

But is the message that business ethics and commercial success can go hand in hand getting through to young people today? From his present position teaching labor studies in several university programs, former United Auto Workers president Douglas Fraser fears that it's not. "I worry about the young people in the graduate school of business," he says. He often finds these students more interested in money and success and less "concerned about the world and its problems" than young people he's taught in other graduate programs.

Nazir Ahmad, however, sees promising signs among his fellow business-school students at Stanford, including the fact that the course on ethics is heavily enrolled. He also feels that, beyond the business community, there is "an increasing recognition that, whether we like business or not, we somehow have to establish a partnership with business in order to deal with larger societal problems."

Yet, as Shirley Williams warns, "one of the things that characterizes the Western world, as distinct from Japan and to some extent even as distinct from one of its members, Germany, is short-termism. Time and again, especially in the Anglo-American world, people are measured by extremely short-term criteria."

The problem, she feels, is particularly acute in business. If a for-profit venture is "going to consider, for example, whether to put money into human or environmental resources—to be a trustee for the next generation—they do it entirely out of the goodness of their hearts. And they do it at risk to their actual measures of success in the hard world of the market.

"I have the impression that in Japan, and to a lesser extent in Germany, there is nothing like the same pressure on the short term." The result, she adds, is that long-term societal goals are more easily attained.

"I remember, for example, a couple of years ago going to the carnival at Mainz [West Germany], and noticing to my surprise that one of the most senior industrialists in Mainz was firmly shown to the fourth row of tables in the Great Hall where the feasts of the carnival were set out. He was very angry and protested very loudly about this. And I asked the mayor of Mainz why he was being shown to this lowly table, and he said, 'Because only half his apprentices passed the exam this year. We wish to show our disapproval of him and the quality of his training.'

"Now, that was a very considerable pressure, a social pressure on business. Those social pressures aren't exercised on business in the same way in the United States or in Britain or in many other Western countries. I think one of the things we need to look at is how one can build into the incentives of our businesses some of the things that would in fact be more helpful to the needs of society and of the environment."

For poet and novelist Brad Leithauser, the problem has particular relevance to the U.S. economy. "I don't see how as a nation we could roll up the deficit we've been rolling up in the past seven years if we honestly believed that the future existed," he says.

"If people as a group believed that in ten years, ten years would have elapsed, and in twenty years, twenty years would have elapsed—if that elementary notion had penetrated people's minds—I don't think what we're doing would be considered acceptable."

The challenges of "short-termism," however, are not unique to the business and financial world. They plague the political sphere as well. "Once we get all the things that we care about on the [political] agenda," says Horner, "I think there's an enormous task of keeping sustained attention on these issues. We've had a terrible history in this country in keeping attention focused."

The problem, she says, is that "we have a boom-and-bust kind of [attention] cycle. The importance of science and math education didn't stop when we got to Sputnik, but in fact it *did* stop in emphasis and attention. So we have to have a series of reports on 'imperiled generations' and 'nations at risk' to even begin to focus on education again. Similarly with poverty. You have a war on poverty, and then you forget that that's an issue."

Whatever the issues we put on the agenda, says Horner, "if we can find a mechanism for sustaining attention and vigilance, it would be wonderful."

Chapter 6

Conclusion

"A mechanism for sustaining attention and vigilance."

In those words, Matina Horner identified the outcome that, well before our conference opened, we had agreed to look for. Such a mechanism wouldn't be an agenda of issues. Agendas, after all, come and go. They prepare the way for solutions, but they aren't themselves the solutions. Nor were we looking for yet another set of pronouncements about the way things ought to be, solemnly agreed to by the conferees and dispatched to yet another rank of dust-gathering shelves.

The right mechanism would have to be, instead, a set of goals, coupled with a set of strategies for realizing them. Properly set, the goals for the year 2000 could become a useful focal point in the remaining decade of the twentieth century, something to keep in view across the intervening years, no matter how much the ship of society pitched and rolled. The strategies, like the gear and tackle of that craft, would provide the mechanism for reaching the goals.

With that in mind, I kept a running list, during our sessions, of everything that sounded like a reasonable goal for the year 2000. Another reporter would no doubt have produced a different list. Since one person's goal is merely another person's strategy for reaching a more distant goal, subjectivity, in listening as in writing, is unavoidable. But any listener would have discerned common themes in the very repetition of items mentioned. Trying to get these on record,

I strove for inclusivity, variety, and specificity. I did, however, set aside some that sounded too much like pious assertions of the "mankind must improve itself" sort. And I quietly deleted some of the motherhood-and-apple-pie goals that have been espoused by every decent society throughout history.

Here, then, is what I heard:

SESSION I

Closing the Gap Between the First and Third World

1. Find ways to measure human welfare other than by GNP per capita.

2. Achieve an adult literacy rate of 85 to 90 percent for each nation.

3. Achieve an average life expectancy of seventy years for each nation.

4. Achieve an infant mortality rate of less than twenty-five deaths per thousand live births for each nation.

5. Achieve an annual population growth rate of 1.0 to 1.5 percent for each nation.

6. Shift from material to human values, emphasizing spiritual and mental development.

7. Reduce the disproportion in share of resources used in North and South.

8. Pay rent, or "conservation easements," for the use of the world's resources.

9. Increase the level of nutrition to a life-sustaining standard.

10. Increase the level of employment across the world to an acceptable level.

11. Provide safe drinking water for every individual.

12. Secure a moderate increase in GNP per capita for each nation.

13. Reduce the numbers of people dropping out of school.

14. Reduce the mortality rate of children under five to seventy per thousand live births (as per the Global Poverty Reduction Act).

15. Achieve a female literacy rate of 80 percent (per the Global Poverty Reduction Act).

16. Reduce the level of absolute poverty to no more than 20 percent of the world's population (per the Global Poverty Reduction Act).

17. Stop the developed world from funding white-elephant projects in Third World nations.

SESSION II

Achieving Peace in a Nuclear Age

18. Adopt a military posture of sufficiency rather than superiority.

19. Nourish the stability of relationships between superpowers.

20. Reduce the share of GNP devoted to military spending.

21. Reduce strategic weaponry by at least 50 percent.

22. Negotiate limits on space-based weapons.

23. Redress the imbalance of conventional arms.

24. Reduce or eliminate nuclear proliferation.

25. Eliminate chemical and biological weapons stockpiling.

26. Agree on reduction of thresholds and frequency of nuclear testing.

27. Develop codes of conduct governing superpower behavior in Third World relationships.

28. Strengthen the role of the United Nations and other multilateral forums.

29. Promote respect for diversity in relationships to the Third World.

30. Improve trust among nations.

31. Increase levels of cultural exchange among nations.

32. Increase the role of young people, women, and rural populations in cultural and diplomatic exchanges.

33. Create new mechanisms for international economic order.

34. Integrate the best things from the socialist and capitalist orders into new economic framework.

35. Encourage the USSR to achieve a 20 percent privatization of its economy.

36. Encourage the USSR to allow at least two candidates for election to stand for every office.

37. Spread the economic benefits of North-South interchanges beyond Third World cities into the rural areas.

38. Publicize changes in the USSR more widely in the Third World.

39. Develop an international Peace Corps.

40. Rise above antagonistic differences between the super-powers.

41. Buy an airplane and take the Wingspread conference to various locations around the world.

42. Affirm the necessity for human rights, so that individuals are no longer tortured for speaking out.

43. Deal with the problem of the underclass in America.

44. Approach the drug problem not as a supply issue but as a demand issue.

45. Eliminate racism and cultural superiority.

46. Alter usage to avoid the word *black* as a term with negative connotations (e.g. "Black Monday").

47. Devise a forum analogous to the economic summit for dealing with world security issues.

48. Develop good indicators for reducing money spent on weapons.

49. Encourage the media to exercise their responsibility to educate rather than simply to entertain.

50. Create multinational teams to address the major issues facing the world.

51. Devise measures that indicate the level of peace in the world.

52. Insist on the free mobility of people wishing to leave their countries.

53. Involve artists more regularly in the formulation of public policy.

54. Produce sitcoms featuring life in the USSR for airing in non-communist nations.

SESSION III

Advancing Civilization: Education, Environment, Quality of Life

55. Engage in satellite mapping of deforestation.

56. Reduce CO_2 buildup to zero.

57. Reduce fossil-fuel burning by 50 percent.

58. Reduce deforestation.

59. Establish global controls on fossil-fuel emissions.

60. Invent governmental systems that can effectively manage resources.

61. Devise a national land-use plan.

62. Develop a set of environmental accounts to assess the productive processes in society.

63. Raise energy taxes in the Western world.

64. Publicize effective models for environmental control.

65. Unify the world by identifying common threats.

66. Invent a new kind of automobile.

67. Provide a liberal education on the nature of technology.

68. Strengthen the United Nations Environment Program.

69. Remove asbestos from schools.

70. Spread education to the masses in the Third World.

71. Capitalize hydropower generation facilities in Africa.

72. Provide clean water.

SESSION IV

Ethics

73. Divide U.S. Social Security checks to indicate proportions coming from prior contributions of the recipient and from welfare of the next generation.

74. Formulate a child's bill of rights.

75. Shift emphasis in schooling from technology to the humanities, poetry, and the arts.

76. Develop a land ethic.

77. Get young people involved in public service in order to instill republican virtues (e.g. equality, self-governance).

78. Make it possible to talk about God in schools.

79. Educate children in the context of one world.

80. Address the results of this conference to the heads of the superpowers.

81. Shift emphasis in education from skills to perspectives.

82. Emphasize in education the necessity for making choices.

83. Inculcate a healthy skepticism for authority.

84. Improve quality of life in cities around the world.

85. Encourage the media to portray the Third World with its dignity intact.

86. Keep sustained attention on these issues.

87. Seek to increase the awareness of the moral behavior of individuals and nations in nuclear and security matters, in the sharing of global resources, and in environmental affairs.

88. Establish a global business ethic.

89. Eliminate apartheid.

90. Make a list of things we don't know much about (e.g. land, cities, drugs).

91. End the foreign occupation of any country.

92. Inculcate a reverence for the future.

93. Encourage accountability of governments.

94. Support fledgling democracies.

95. Abandon superpower support for oppressive governments.

This, then, is the initial list. Its order reflects the way in which these ideas spilled out onto the table. It includes some wonderfully odd ideas, like Andrei Voznesensky's proposal for buying an airliner to carry our conference to various sites in the Third World and in communist nations. It comprises ideas that are repetitious (numbers 11 and 72, for instance, dealing with clean water). It lists proposals that are highly generalized ("Improve trust among nations," number 30), and suggestions so precise that experts will immediately argue over their targets ("Reduce fossil-fuel burning by 50 percent," number 57). And it comprises some ideas that have, happily, begun to be overtaken by events: As this book goes to press, Mikhail Gorbachev has already addressed the

United Nations and laid out his promises for troop withdrawals in Europe and new freedoms within the Soviet Union, and the thirty-five-nation Conference on Security and Cooperation in Europe, meeting in Vienna, has approved a broad-gauge document specifying new ranges of human rights.

Rather than trim the list in light of these developments, however, it has been allowed to stand, not simply as a monument to a few days' discussion but out of a conviction that our conference, if its usefulness is to be felt beyond the walls of Wingspread, must provide the raw materials upon which individual readers can build their own thinking. Expert conclusions are useful, to be sure. Where we could, we provided them. But the real purpose here is to set forth a kind of citizens' guide to the Year 2000: a kaleidoscope of ideas which, by dint of a little turning, the reader can combine in ways our conferees never even glimpsed.

On the last morning of our conference, as the suitcases began collecting by the front door and the airport-bound station wagons began drawing up on the pebbled circular drive, the conferees gathered for a final session. We then broke up into four small committees, according to the four broad topics we had been considering. Our task: to extract from the list of ninety-five ideas those that seemed both the most pressing and the most do-able. Sifting goals from the mechanisms for reaching them, we prefaced each short list with an articulation of the problem, and then appended to each a list of strategies.

Here, under four headings, are what we took to be the reasonable goals for the year 2000. If these four sets are not precisely parallel, that should come as no surprise. They were not all cut from the same fabric. They range from the obvious to the unexpected, from the precisely numerical to the highly abstract. Why? In part because the following statements were drafted by four separate committees, each comprising individuals with differing experiences, differing capacities for hope and concern, and differing concepts of what may or may not be "reasonable."

In part, too, they differ because they reflect diverse intellectual traditions. Development economics, for example— the discipline underlying much of the discussion of the North-South gap—has been shaped along lines quite different from those shaping East-West diplomacy, characterized by careful calibration and subtle political nuance. And those two, in turn, speak a language rather different from that of the environmental movement—born in grass-roots protest, and only recently come of age—or the centuries-old tradition of ethical and philosophical discourse.

Finally, they differ because some of them, quite frankly, are not set up merely to be reached, though reaching them matters a great deal. They are meant to do more: to provoke, to expand limits, to steer thought into new channels, to stir the sort of endeavor that eventually exceeds the mark and sets even tougher goals.

Here, in the prose of the committees that wrote them, are the four statements of goals:

THE NORTH-SOUTH GAP

I. Conference Statement

Per capita gross national product (GNP) has been the traditional means of measuring national progress. The goal of raising per capita GNP has guided international development programs. Such programs have failed. The gap between rich and poor countries has grown, and within many countries the gap between rich and poor groups has widened. Absolute poverty has increased.

Development efforts can be refocused to address human well-being more directly. Data increasingly available can be used to provide more useful measuring criteria. These must include clear, easily understood descriptions of the human condition so that programs can be designed and improvement in the human condition can be easily assessed and compared from nation to nation.

II. Achievable goals

While each nation must set its own goals, a developing country that achieves the following will have closed the gap with the developed world in satisfying basic needs:

1. An infant mortality rate of less than twenty-five deaths per thousand live births.

2. A population growth rate of less than 1 percent per year.

3. An adult literacy rate of 85 percent.

4. Life expectancy of seventy years.

5. Meaningful employment of the greatest number possible.

III. Strategies for progress

1. Redirect the development strategies of the developing countries, as well as the policies of the bilateral and multilateral development institutions, away from exclusive reliance on economic factors.

2. Design, implement, and track development programs using these new criteria.

3. Continue to emphasize the obligations of the developed nations to help improve economic growth and overall economic performance in the developing countries. But

target each nation's internal development effort, as well as cooperative international efforts, on the fulfillment of the noneconomic goals.

4. Recognize that this new way of thinking about development will require a major effort on the part of developing countries, as well as significant increases in and transfers of resources from the developed countries.

EAST-WEST RELATIONS

I. Conference Statement

The superpower conflict has led to the development of nuclear arsenals that place at risk the survival not only of the nations of the East and West but of all other nations. The intensity of this conflict has not only distorted the economic and social priorities of East and West but has adversely affected the ways in which the superpowers relate to the countries of the nonaligned world, particularly the developing nations.

Recently, however, there has been a dramatic shift in the Soviet leadership's approach to its domestic problems and international relationships. There has also been a shift in the West toward greater receptivity to cooperative ventures with the Soviets. As a result, there appears to be a greater openness and tolerance on both sides, leading to a greater capacity to cooperate, than at any time since World War II.

II. Achievable goals

1. Return to a world without nuclear weaponry, in so far as achievable.

2. Move toward confidence-building measures that reduce political tensions between East and West.

3. Move from a posture of mistrust, competition, and fear to a posture of cooperation.

4. Engage both the West and East in assisting the developing nations to attain peace and eradicate poverty.

III. Strategies for progress

1. Reduce superpower engagement in regional conflicts, especially those involving low-intensity warfare.

2. Strengthen the United Nations and regional organizations to deal with peacekeeping functions.

3. Move beyond the prospective 50 percent reduction in strategic nuclear weapons toward further agreements to reduce nuclear and conventional arms and to reduce and eliminate nuclear testing.

4. Strengthen the impediments to proliferation of nuclear weapons among nonnuclear states.

5. Create new restraints to the conventional arms trade among nations.

6. Encourage negotiated settlements of conflicts, and support the application of sanctions against nations tolerating international terrorism.

7. Ban the development, production, stockpiling, and use of biological and chemical weapons.

8. Increase economic cooperation through expanding trade and investment.

9. Increase possibilities of nongovernmental cultural exchange, including:

- exchange of students, scholars, and young people;
- sharing of artistic endeavors; and
- use of television and film to convey realistic views of life in each country and to promote understanding.

ENVIRONMENTAL DEGRADATION

I. Conference Statement

The planet Earth has finite resources and a fragile atmosphere. It is under increasing pressure because of rising population and industrialization and the consequent destruction of resources and pollution of the environment. The quality of life of individuals and societies depends upon sustaining a healthy environment.

Both the scale and the pace of transformation of the environment by human activities have been rapidly expanding. This expansion has pushed the environmental issues squarely onto the agendas of our newly interconnected global society. The result is an increasing awareness of the relationship between environmental protection and social well-being, an awareness that provides new opportunities for constructive action.

II. Achievable goals

1. Create national plans within each nation for the sustainable use of the land. While sustainable land use is probably not attainable by the year 2000 in every nation, it is possible to develop a plan for such use and a timetable for its implementation.

2. Establish a planetary trust for the conservation of living resources at levels adequate to preserve regional and global life-support systems. Such a planetary trusteeship would

allow the world's populations as a whole to determine priorities for the protection of particular resources, habitats, species, and so forth.

3. Achieve a reduction in the rates of fossil fuel use that is sufficient to stabilize and ultimately reverse environmental degradation across a range of issues, including the global warming trend, air and water pollution, acid rain, toxic wastes, and the buildup of nondegradable pollutants in the soil.

III. Strategies for progress

1. Establish an international system of environmental accounts, modeled on current economic accounts and designed to assess such issues as cross-national exchanges of pollutants, activities of multinational corporations, and other transboundary issues.

2. Strengthen international environmental institutions, both governmental and nongovernmental. These institutions should perform the environmental accounting tasks, provide mixed-nation research teams for basic fact-finding and analysis, and establish the computer modeling necessary for sound accounting.

3. Establish a system of global rents for the conservation of living natural resources, with payments scaled to the GNP of the contributing nations.

4. Vigorously pursue the research, development, and funding of alternatives to fossil-fuel energy sources.

5. Increase the worldwide prices of fossil fuels, through taxes or other means, to levels more consistent with the costs that their continued use imposes on environmental protection.

ETHICS

I. Conference Statement

As the world becomes increasingly interdependent, the concept of relationships—among individuals, families, communities, nations—is replacing the concept of rigid self-reliance and isolationism as a paradigm for human enterprise. Successful relationships cannot be fully legislated. They depend, in part, on mutual adherence to widely shared but unenforceable sets of values. Yet today, paradoxically, attention to these moral dimensions of human behavior seems to be waning.

Just as individuals cannot remain unaffected by their communities, so nations can no longer successfully opt out of the global context. Major transnational problems cannot be solved by single nations. Increasingly, individuals and nations need to find ethical ways to balance their own rights and entitlements with their obligations and responsibilities to others, and to bring ethical considerations to bear on every aspect of private and public relationships.

II. Achievable goals

1. Increase awareness among individuals and nations of the moral dimensions of behavior.

2. Articulate and support codes of ethics for international business.

3. Develop educational curricula that reflect the realities of global interdependence.

4. Inculcate a reverence for the future.

5. Increase awareness of the holistic nature of global problems and their possible solutions.

III. Strategies for progress

1. Establish compulsory basic education on a global scale.

2. Within the education systems of each nation, teach the values required both to realize individual potential and to establish meaningful interpersonal relations and sound global policies.

3. Encourage creativity by balancing sound technological education and an emphasis on the arts and humanities.

4. Establish a child's bill of rights.

5. Promote community service as a means of inculcating a sense of caring and sharing.

6. Within each individual and nation, and among individuals and nations, balance entitlements and obligations in political, economic, cultural, social, and legal spheres.

7. Support the development of a global syllabus of issues that affect every individual, tailored to local needs but holistic in conception.

8. Work to channel human energies—including moral outrage over such issues as political tyranny, racial discrimination, greed, and selfishness—into constructive patterns of reform.

છ∾

Those, as we saw them, were the reasonable goals for the year 2000. Now what?

If the world were a simpler place, one might say that it contains two sorts of people: those who believe in conferences, and those who don't. Into the former camp would fall the majority: those who believe that progress depends upon consensus, and that consensus arises most efficiently through conversation, debate, argument, and the results of serendipitous but stimulating human interchange. Into the latter camp would fall a minority: those who look with great suspicion on committees of all sorts, who favor individual initiative, and who are convinced that the work of the world best gets done by giving the solitary mind enough space to think its way to solutions unimpeded by others.

Conferences comprising only the latter sort would, of course, collapse the moment they began. But meetings of only the former would be at risk of overstating their own importance. Every good conference needs the leaven of that skeptical minority: the voice, usually lonely and often contrarian, of the reluctant conference-goer wondering what good can possibly come from yet another bunch of people sitting around a table.

At Wingspread that voice came—politely and respectfully, to be sure, but clearly articulated—from Tina Rosenberg. An American journalist living in Santiago, Chile, she has also spent time in Managua writing, she told us, about "how societies and their culture and their history shape what people do and how they behave, and whether those things are changeable or not." Youthful, reserved, alert, she confessed to being a novice at attending conferences. At the sessions themselves, she spoke up only a few times. Her points, however, so caught the attention of the room by their honesty and directness that the remaining discussion was peppered with allusions to "what Tina said."

Her initial question, addressed to Rodrigo Botero during the opening evening session, was in fact meant for us all. "I think maybe I'm missing the point of what you're saying," she said at the conclusion of his opening presentation on goals for North-South relations. "What makes what you're saying more than an accounting trick, just sort of declaring the war won? What are the real differences that your goals are going to make?"

The conversation moved on. But the essence of the question remained: What difference will it all make? The following day she put it more directly.

"This is the first real conference that I've ever been to," she noted candidly, "and I've met a lot of interesting people and I've had a lot of great conversations. But I don't understand the purpose of the conference. I don't understand what contribution we are making to the world by providing a list of things that we can all agree on and that would be nice things for the world to have.

"One thing I'm struck by is how much agreement there is on the things we're saying. Everybody has terrific ideas— which sort of indicates that this may not be the most useful way of going about it. We've all had these ideas for a while, and many of us have tried to work on our ideas, and we know what the limitations are. I just don't understand the purpose of this list of wonderful things."

What she was raising, in fact, was one of the world's most useful questions: *So what?* So a group of thoughtful people arrive at a list of global goals for the year 2000: So what? So they refine them, develop strategies to pursue them, and publish them widely: So what? Is there, in the end, anything to show for all that work? How does that change the world?

Amitai Etzioni spoke to that cosmic *So what?* when he noted that "It's not enough to articulate the right goals." Just as an agenda needs specific goals, so the goals need to be embodied in action, a point made forcefully by Shirley Williams. "If we have nothing but list after list of desirable ends," she observed, "none of them will happen."

How does a struggling world make them happen? How can we ensure that the year 2000 does not simply drown in accumulated lists and reports? Woven through the discussions were references to at least four different mechanisms for stimulating action.

The first and most obvious is the tried-and-true response of humanity whenever it looks for ways forward: identify and use existing institutions. After some goals have been set, says Gail Lapidus, "it seems to me that our concern ought to be how to get these issues onto the political agenda of other institutions, and, if there aren't those institutions, how to begin to think about creating them." Several institutions already exist:

Governments. Commanding large resources, governments generally operate with significant public support. Yet "one of the great problems we have," says Shirley Williams, "is to make [these goals] grip on national governments." The challenge among Western democracies is the short-term nature of political thinking geared to the next election. Among developing-world governments, challenges range from the lack of mechanisms for addressing problems to a poverty-driven desperation more worried about surviving today than considering tomorrow—and on to an all-absorbing nationalism that seeks to assert itself whatever the cost. Nevertheless, the institution ultimately empowered to help humanity reach many of its goals is government.

Nongovernment organizations. Often specialized in nature, such groups are typically part of the not-for-profit sector in Western nations—and are just beginning to make their presence felt in the Communist nations, as evidenced in the fledgling movement toward private philanthropy in the Soviet Union. They can have strong grass-roots ties, years of experience in solving local problems, and long-term commitments. Many, however, lack an umbrella of common goals linking them with similar organizations around the world. They do, however, have tremendous potential for mobilizing political will behind certain clearly defined objectives.

The news media. Both by choice of stories and by the angle given them, the world's media helps set agendas, promote goals, and publicize solutions. Its influence is often dissipated by concentration on personality and sensationalism— and by scanty or biased reporting, especially on issues in the developing world. But its commitment to digging for answers and its ability to endow even far-off and seemingly marginal issues with relevance make it an obvious leader in the march toward global goals.

Foundations. Major philanthropic foundations are increasingly interested in global issues. Gail Lapidus describes them as "another powerful force in charting new paths, in crossing traditional boundaries, in opening new questions, and in devoting resources toward examining them and getting them on the political agenda." Foundations rarely have the resources to engage in broad-based, long-term delivery of services. But they are often useful in providing seed money and in spearheading the larger involvements of government and private enterprise.

The second way forward, an obvious adjunct to the search for existing institutions, is the invention of new ones. While existing institutions contribute significantly to global advancement, they leave obvious gaps, sometimes because they are too nationalistic, too specialized, or too small. Hence the need for new ones. This process of invention, says William Clark, may sometimes be effective simply by developing larger versions of existing mechanisms. "We have a number of models or experiments that have worked at some scales," he notes. "We have to see how they work at different scales."

111

He cites as an example the establishment of a regional watershed or "airshed" association to determine the level of stress on a local environment and determine appropriate controls, an idea that could be extended, he feels, to deal with global environmental issues. "In very halting, very incomplete ways," he says, "we are beginning to invent these fora."

Also being invented are new ways of connecting interested groups with one another. New forms of advertising, increasingly sophisticated technologies for computer networking, and more broad-based methodologies for fund-raising are all contributing to a growing sense of global interdependence and a growing body of individuals concerned with global issues.

And that, quite naturally, leads to a third approach for reaching humanity's goals, which is to involve individuals through volunteer efforts. "You have to worry about how to [carry out] this idea of empowering people and involving them," says Amitai Etzioni. Or, as Bill Clark puts it, "We have to create a forum which is driven by public opinion itself."

Here the nature of the goals selected becomes particularly important. A quick, appealing goal—on the order of the 1985 Live Aid concert, a global event designed to raise money to help end famine in Africa—may excite immediate support without building a base for concerted, ongoing action. On the other hand, goals that are too lofty will prove fruitless. "Psychologically," says Rodrigo Botero, "for an individual, and I think for a country, if you offer a goal that becomes unreachable, the natural human reaction will be to reject that goal because you're testing that person, that [nation], against an impossible goal."

When the right goals are set, however, the resulting involvement of individuals can be significant and impressive. A 1988 report from Independent Sector, a Washington-based coalition of corporate, foundation, and volunteer groups, estimates that nearly 50 percent of Americans volunteer, with twenty-three million giving five or more hours per week. Such volunteering often begins with asking two questions squarely addressed by the conferees at Wingspread: What are the most pressing issues, and what goals can I set for my own contribution?

Ultimately, however, these three mechanisms will only be effective if they lead to a fourth, all-embracing result: the change of individual attitudes that helps generate the political will to address serious problems. Andrei Voznesensky, reflecting on developments in the Soviet Union, spoke of a "revolution in consciousness." Others talked about the need to overcome antagonism, develop better communications, build more trust, exercise deeper commitments, and foster more caring among individuals.

Such qualities, many feel, must characterize the interrelations among nations, too. But a nation embodies the thinking of its citizenry: Only as individuals exhibit sound qualities of thought and action will nations prosper. To be sure, nations may often be more than the sums of their parts. But those parts—the citizens whose lives shape and reflect the collective will of the nation—form the core of values upon which a nation stands. If global goals are to be reached, the thinking of the citizenry must first find them reachable, desirable, and worth striving for.

And that, it seems, provides the raison d'être for conferences such as ours: to encourage that progress, to help change thinking. Judging from the discussions around our table, that was our ultimate goal, the final answer to the great *So what?*

Changing thinking, however, is not synonymous with changing personalities. Among the assumptions apparently shared around the table was the conviction that the world is not, ultimately, driven by personalities—that the personalities arise either to lead nations forward or to tyrannize over them in proportion as the thinking of the citizenry is enlightened or enslaved. Nor did our group seem wedded to the notion that what drives human progress is either events or institutions. Those, too, are reflections rather than causes.

Instead, our group seemed intent on searching out ideas, in finding the warp and woof of thought as it arises in individual understanding, spreads itself across societies, lets itself be shaped by others' thought, and determines the standards whereby personalities, events, and institutions are seen to be unthinkable or inevitable, intolerable or acceptable. If we agreed on any single concept, it is that the tenor of thought will largely shape humanity's disposition to strive for or ignore the goals for the year 2000.

And that, I find, is cause for great encouragement. Looking back, I see those April days in Racine not as days of pessimism but of hope. True, the world seemed to be coming unzipped. True, the future was beset with snares and danger signs. But if thought itself is the great determinant of the future — if British novelist John Galsworthy was right in noting that "If you do not think about the future, you cannot have one" — then there is reason for at least a cautious optimism. Thought, after all, can be changed, if we're willing to make the effort.

Making that effort, in these closing years of the century, has become the unavoidable task of humanity. A half century ago, Albert Einstein commented on the power of thought in a sentence that has become almost a cliché among peace activists. "The unleashed power of the atom has changed everything save our modes of thinking," he wrote, "and thus we drift toward unparalleled catastrophe." His conclusion, one hopes, may no longer be quite so self-evident as it seemed during the days of the Cold War. But his premise — that technology rushes brazenly onstage while thought lingers timidly in the wings—is accurate.

The purpose of our conference? It was not, in retrospect, to dwell on "unparalleled catastrophe." It was to address "our modes of thinking"—with the assurance that they could be and must be adjusted. We set out to establish goals for the year 2000 not simply for the sake of *reaching* them (although that itself would be of inestimable benefit to society) but for the sake of the shifts of thought that would occur along the way. In proportion as those shifts happen to individuals everywhere, in all walks of life, and in every degree of depth and sophistication, the year 2000 will be characterized, in the words Adam Yarmolinsky used to sum up the Wingspread conference, by "a vivid appreciation of the lack of limits for human aspiration." There is, I suppose, no goal more worth attaining.

Appendices

In preparation for the Wingspread conference, "Agenda 2000: Reasonable Goals," the cosponsors commissioned three papers by conference participants on the major subject areas under consideration. These papers appear here.

Rodrigo Botero's paper, titled "The Gap Between Developed and Developing Countries: Changing Perceptions," appears essentially as submitted. Mr. Botero, former finance minister of Colombia, is currently at Harvard's Center for National Affairs and is a Ford Foundation trustee.

Gail W. Lapidus's paper, titled "Gorbachev's Reforms and the Future of East-West Relations," is an edited version of her original submission, which appeared as "Gorbachev and the Reform of the Soviet System" in *Daedalus* 116, no. 2 (Spring 1987), 1–30. Permission from Stephen R. Graubard and the American Academy of Arts and Sciences to republish her paper is gratefully acknowledged. Professor Lapidus is chair of the Berkeley-Stanford Program on Soviet International Behavior and a professor of political science at the University of California-Berkeley.

Peter H. Raven's paper, "State of the World, 2000: What We Should Do to Affect It," is an edited version of his original submission. Dr. Raven, director of the Missouri Botanical Garden and Engelmann Professor of Botany at Washington University, is Home Secretary of the National Academy of Sciences.

The Gap between Developed
and Developing Countries:
Changing Perceptions

Rodrigo Botero

Any reasonable listing of foreseeable international issues at the beginning of the next century would probably include the problems of the poor countries and their relations with that part of humanity that can be described as affluent. Should present trends provide a reliable guide to the future, it would appear that, by the time an infant born this year comes of age, the question of whether his or her country of residence can be classified as industrialized or underdeveloped may turn out to be one of the most relevant determinants of opportunity and overall well-being for that person as an adult.

That consideration explains why the struggle for development can be expected to receive high priority from national governments as well as the international community in the years to come, even in the absence of a consensus with respect to how best to achieve the desired objective. In fact, the improvement of the living conditions of the two thirds of the earth's population that constitutes the Third World has been a major international issue since the decade of the 1950s. That this issue should still remain on the world's agenda in the 21st century speaks eloquently of its importance. In retrospect, it also reminds us that the task of social and economic modernization has turned out to be much more complex and difficult than it initially appeared. The intractability of underdevelopment, the frustrations and setbacks experienced

117

in the development process, the magnitude of the mistakes that have been committed in the quest for economic growth, all put a premium on modesty and caution with respect to what can be expected. Not many responsible experts are willing to use the expression "development decade" as a meaningful concept nowadays. The relevant time period for a developing country to be launched on the path of self-sustaining growth is better expressed in terms of generations. And as the noneconomic aspects of the development process are more fully taken into account, the perception of the true magnitude of the task has changed.

Can the gap between developed and developing countries be closed in the foreseeable future? The question is certainly not a new one. In one way or another, it has been at the root of the thinking about "economic development" ever since the term was incorporated into academic parlance and, shortly thereafter, into the terminology of politics and diplomacy. Expressions such as "emerging nations," "developing countries," and "stages of economic growth" convey a sense of dynamism, of inherent optimism in the advancement of progress. This underlying confidence in progress reflects an attitude that was prevalent some thirty years ago, not without reason. By the end of the decade of the 1950s, Western Europe had rebuilt its economy and was well on its way towards prosperity; Japan was about to join the ranks of the industrialized democracies; the process of decolonization was in full sway; and world trade was expanding. There was plenty of tangible evidence of the remarkable achievements brought about by the judicious combination of technology, financial resources, and modern management skills: the recovery from the destruction of World War II, the United Nations system, the Bretton Woods institutions (the World Bank and the International Monetary Fund), jet propulsion, the electronic revolution, the beginning of space exploration. If these formidable achievements had been accomplished successfully, it did not at the time seem unrealistic to evaluate the prospects for the modernization of the underdeveloped world with a certain degree of optimism. The leadership of the industrialized Western powers had ample reason for entertaining a sense of satisfaction with past performance, and of confidence in the capacity to meet future challenges with similar success.

In the new nations of Asia and Africa, there were high hopes that, along with political independence, economic prosperity and other good things would follow. As a result, the task of launching the underdeveloped world on the path of self-sustaining growth received strong support from the international community for a brief period. During a few years there existed, on the part of the developed and the developing countries, an agreement that the development effort, as a priority issue on the world's agenda, merited substantial international support. At that time, the answer to the question of the feasibility of closing the gap between rich and poor nations would probably have been in the affirmative — with qualifications as to the time required for individual cases, taking into account the different categories of underdevelopment.

The attitude of self-confidence and commitment to progress on the part of the industrialized countries was reflected in the belief that economic development was the natural path of all underdeveloped nations. The differences would be in the *how* and the *when*. But the end result would be worldwide development. Projections were made as to how long it would take different countries to reach the category of "developed," on the basis of a given annual rate of growth. Scenarios were built on the premise of eventual affluence for all of humanity. According to one futurologist who had participated in this kind of exercise, universal affluence had only a few drawbacks: He estimated, for example, that at any given moment there would be over two million visitors in the Sistine Chapel.

Subsequent events did not quite correspond to initial expectations. Toward the end of the 1960s, an international commission chaired by Lester Pearson, former prime minister of Canada, reported on the crisis in aid. After evaluating the consequences of twenty years of development assistance, it concluded:

> The widening gap between the developed and developing countries has become a central issue of our time.
> The effort to reduce it has inspired the nations left behind by the technological revolution to mobilize their resources for economic growth. It has also produced a transfer of resources on an unprecedented scale from richer to poorer countries. International cooperation for development over the last twenty years has been of a nature and on a scale new to history.
> The attempt to do something about this gap was based on the assumption that economic under-development would yield to a determined national effort to change it, with external help from those whose economic strength made this possible. The transfer of resources that gave substance to this international cooperative effort began after the war and increased rapidly in the late 1950's. By 1961, almost 8 billion dollars, or nearly 1 per cent of the Gross National Product (GNP) of the high-income, non-Communist nations was flowing into low-income nations. . . . However, international support for development is now flagging. In some of the rich countries its feasibility, even its purpose, is in question. The climate surrounding foreign aid programs is heavy with disillusion and distrust. This is not true everywhere. Indeed, there are countries in which the opposite is true. Nevertheless, we have reached a point of crisis.[1]

By this time, the agreement between rich and poor countries concerning the development effort was being eroded by the disparity between initial expectations and actual results.

In the developed countries, signs of "aid fatigue" were appearing in the form of increasing political opposition to international cooperation. In the developing countries, certain aspects of the donor-recipient relationship were being questioned with increasing assertiveness. By the middle of the 1970s, what remained of the consensus in the international community concerning development issues was devastated by the combined effects of the Vietnam War, the oil shock, and the 1973 recession, which brought to an end a quarter-century of postwar expansion of the world economy. The conversation between rich and poor countries (or North-South debate, as it came to be called) turned into an acrimonious exchange of recriminations at the headquarters of the United Nations and at other international fora.

It would go beyond the scope of this paper to attempt to summarize or to judge the arguments put forth with increasing stridency by representatives of North and South trying to assign the blame for the economic hardship then being experienced by the developed countries as well as the nonoil-developing countries. As antagonisms hardened, and as the debate was taken over by politicians and diplomats, one side referred to the greed of OPEC and the incompetence of the developing country leadership, while the other side replied by pointing out the inequities in the international economy and the selfishness of the industrialized country governments. By then, the assumption of a shared interest in the development effort had been transformed into an adversarial relationship, where conflict between North and South was taken for granted. Furthermore, the focus on the issue of the eventual closing of the gap between developed and developing countries was now shifting, as the relevance of such an objective was questioned.

A World Bank study on the experience of twenty-five years of economic development described some of the successes as well as the failures of the 1950–1975 period.[2]

On the basis of past performance, a projection was made for all the developing countries with populations of one million or more whose growth rate of per capita income had exceeded that of the industrialized countries during 1960–1975. The aim was to estimate how long it would take for each one of them to close the income gap with the rich countries, measured in dollars per person per year (see Table 1). Only three of the countries listed — Libya, Saudi Arabia, and Singapore — were expected to close the gap before the end of this century. The estimated waiting periods for the others ranged from thirty-seven years for Israel to a sobering 3,224 years for Mauritania. In the light of such numbers, the question that seems to follow is that of the usefulness of such an exercise as a guide to policy-making. As the author of the study points out:

> Fortunately, there are compelling reasons to believe that most developing countries will not place the closing of the gap at the center of their aspirations. First, not all of them regard the resource-wasting life style of the developed countries as an end toward which it is worth striving; at least some seem to prefer to create their own development patterns based on their own resources, and needs, and traditions.
>
> Second, when thinking of the per-capita income that they would like to attain, most people (and governments) tend to think of the income of a close-by reference group. Thus, for example, despite the fact that within most countries there is a clear positive association between income and self-rated happiness, there is no observable tendency for people in poor countries to rate themselves as less happy on average than people in rich countries rate themselves.... There are several possible explanations of this apparent paradox .... One of them is simply that most people in poor countries do not regard the rich foreigners as part of their reference group and hence are not overconcerned with the gap. They are more concerned, it

seems, with their own internal income distributions and their own place within them.[3]

By the time the Brandt Commission (the Independent Commission on International Development Issues, chaired by former West German chancellor Willy Brandt) issued its report on development issues in 1980, new trends in the world economy were reshaping the relations between developed and developing countries—as well as the relations between different categories of developing countries. The massive transfer of wealth to the oil-exporting countries during the 1970s had created a new group of rich countries within the South. These countries were members of the Organization of Petroleum Exporting Countries (OPEC). They had become rich without becoming "developed" in terms of their industrial capacity, the technical or scientific advancement of their population, or their political and institutional structures.

In addition, another group of advanced developing countries in East Asia and Latin America were industrializing rapidly and becoming successful exporters of manufactures. At the other extreme, the group of least-developed countries—located mostly in sub-Saharan Africa and South Asia—was falling further behind the rest of the world.

Given the heterogeneity of the developing countries, their various income levels, and their differing growth performance, it was becoming more difficult to describe their situation accurately by placing them all under the same category. Once the differences between groups of developing countries were also taken into account, the issue of the gap had become more complicated (Table 2), as the authors of the Brandt Report made plain:

The crisis through which international relations and the world economy are now passing presents great dangers, and they appear to be growing more serious. We believe that the

123

gap which separates rich and poor countries—a gap so wide that at the extremes people seem to live in different worlds— has not been sufficiently recognized as a major factor in this crisis. It is a great contradiction of our age that these dispari- ties exist—and are in some respects widening—just when hu- man society is beginning to have a clearer perception of how it is interrelated and of how North and South depend on each other in a single world economy. . . .

There are obvious objections to a simplified view of the world as being divided into two camps. The "North" includes two rich industrialized countries south of the equator, Austra- lia and New Zealand. The "South" ranges from a booming half-industrial nation like Brazil to poor landlocked or island countries such as Chad or the Maldives. A few southern coun- tries—mostly oil-exporters—have higher per capita incomes than some of the northern countries. But in general terms, and although neither is a uniform or permanent grouping, "North" and "South" are broadly synonymous with "rich" and "poor," "developed" and "developing." [4]

From today's perspective, however, taking into account the development experience of the last four decades, one can question the validity of statements or forecasts that apply to all of the developing countries. Expressions such as "the South," "the Third World," or "the Group of 77" that have now entered the language of diplomacy and of journalism de- scribe a large and disparate group of countries with enormous differences in outlook, in culture, and in development experi- ence. There is at present no such thing as a development model that all developing countries recognize as successful and worthy of being universally adopted. Some countries pre- fer a market economy; others prefer a centrally planned econ- omy. Some are trying to follow a modernization strategy similar to that of the industrialized Western powers; others reject that alternative and stress the supremacy of funda- mentalist religion and traditional values. Some are export- oriented; others are inward-looking. In brief, there are now a multitude of development models that are being tried out as different societies attempt to respond to the challenge of modernization.

Rather than attempting to predict the outcome of that competition by the year 2000, it seems more useful to refer to an element of the development dialogue that should remain relevant for all countries regardless of their economic or political differences: the reduction of absolute poverty.

If the question of the narrowing of the gap between rich and poor countries is focused on the qualitative aspects of human welfare—education, nutrition, life expectancy, infant mortality—a more hopeful picture emerges than that which is provided by the comparisons of GNP per capita. The development experience of the last four decades demonstrates that—thanks to modern science and readily available methods of delivery of basic services in health care, nutrition, primary education, family planning, water supply, and sewage disposal—a developing country can substantially reduce the welfare gap with the developed countries even while the absolute gap in GNP per capita is still large.

At a relatively modest level of GNP per capita, with a sustained commitment to social objectives, it is possible to obtain an adult literacy rate of 85 to 90 percent, an average life expectancy of seventy years, an infant mortality rate of less than twenty-five deaths per thousand live births, and a population growth rate of 1 to 1.5 percent per year.

These over-all indicators of social well-being are comparable to the average levels of the industrialized countries today, but more favorable than the levels of well-being that the industrialized countries had in the first decades of this century. These levels of well-being have already been reached by countries such as Barbados, Chile, Costa Rica, Cuba, and Korea, notwithstanding their differences in size and in political organization. If similar levels of social well-being were to be reached by all developing countries by the year 2000, humanity would have taken a gigantic step towards the elimination of suffering and deprivation.

Although these are more modest goals, they may be more meaningful ones than the attempt to close the gap in GNP per capita between the rich and the poor nations.

Table 1 THE ABSOLUTE GAP: WHEN MIGHT IT BE CLOSED? [a]

Country	GNP per capita, 1975 (in 1974 U.S. dollars) [b]	Annual growth rate, 1960–75 (percent)	Years to close gap at 1960–75 growth rate
OECD countries	5,238	3.7	—
Libyan Arab Republic	4,675	11.8	2
Saudi Arabia	2,767	8.6	14
Singapore	2,307	7.6	22
Israel	3,287	5.0	37
Iran	1,321	6.9	45
Hong Kong	1,584	6.3	48
Korea	504	7.3	69
China (Taiwan)	817	6.3	75
Iraq	1,180	4.4	223
Brazil	927	4.2	362
Thailand	319	4.5	365
Tunisia	695	4.2	422
Syrian Arab Republic	604	4.2	451
Lesotho	161	4.5	454
Turkey	793	4.0	675
Togo	245	4.1	807
Panama	977	3.8	1,866
Malawi	137	3.9	1,920
Malaysia	665	3.8	2,293
Papua New Guinea	412	3.8	2,826
China (People's Republic)	320	3.8	2,900
Mauritania	288	3.8	3,224

a. Absolute gap is GNP per capita of the OECD countries ($2,378 in 1950, $5,238 in 1975) less GNP per capita of the individual country.

b. All developing countries with population of 1 million or more whose growth rate of per capita income exceeded that of the OECD countries during 1960–75.

Source: Computed from data tapes, World Bank Atlas (1977).

Transcribed from: David Morawetz, *Twenty-five Years of Economic Development, 1950 to 1975.* Washington, D.C.; World Bank Books, 1977.

Table 2 COMPARISONS BETWEEN DEVELOPED COUNTRIES AND
DIFFERENT CATEGORIES OF DEVELOPING COUNTRIES:
BASIC INDICATORS

| Countries | 1985 population (in millions) | GNP PER CAPITA | | Life expectancy at birth, 1985 |
		1985 U.S. dollars	Average annual growth rate (percent) 1965–1985	
Industrial market economies				
United States	239	16690	1.7	76
Japan	121	11300	4.7	77
United Kingdom	56	8460	1.6	75
Spain	39	4290	2.6	77
High-income oil exporters				
Libya	4	7170	-1.3	60
Saudi Arabia	12	8850	5.3	62
Kuwait	2	14480	-0.3	72
Upper middle-income				
Brazil	136	1640	4.3	65
Korea	41	2150	6.6	69
Portugal	10	1970	3.3	74
Lower middle-income				
Indonesia	162	530	4.8	55
Thailand	52	800	4.0	64
Egypt	48	610	3.1	61
Turkey	50	1080	2.6	64
Colombia	28	1320	2.9	65
Low-income economies				
China	1040	310	4.8	69
India	765	270	1.7	56
Bangladesh	101	150	0.4	51
Ethiopia	42	110	0.2	45
Pakistan	96	380	2.6	51
Zaire	31	170	-2.1	51

SOURCE: *World Development Report 1987,* Oxford University Press, June 1987; World Bank, Washington, D.C.

Gorbachev's Reforms
and the Future of
East-West Relations

Gail W. Lapidus[1]

A dramatic struggle is under way in the Soviet Union today, a struggle not only over the reform of prevailing institutions and policies but, as the poet Andrei Voznesensky recently put it, one which involves a "revolution in consciousness" within the Soviet elite.

Despite striking parallels to Khrushchev's earlier campaign for de-Stalinization and the reform of the Soviet system, the scope of Gorbachev's effort is potentially more vast and its thrust rather different. At issue are not merely the errors of a single leader, however significant the role he played, but the very nature of the system he shaped and its capacity to address effectively both the internal and the international demands of the 1980s and beyond. His campaign for *perestroika* ("restructuring") is a call for far-reaching departures from prevailing practices and norms across virtually every area of Soviet life. Its success would entail radical changes, not only in the organization of the Soviet economy, but also in social and cultural policy, in Soviet political life, and ultimately in the way in which the Soviet Union deals with the larger international community.

It is tempting to view current developments in the Soviet Union through the prism of Russian history. Over several centuries, international weakness or military defeat has repeatedly served as a catalyst for internal reform, and

Gorbachev can plausibly be portrayed as the latest in a long tradition of reforming tsar-autocrats, from Peter the Great to Stalin, seeking to impose radical and coercive modernization from above on a passive, backward, and recalcitrant society. While this analogy is not altogether wide of the mark, it fails to capture the extent to which current efforts at reform are a belated response to fundamental economic and social changes which have altered the relationship of state and society in Russia. The current attempt at reform is only partially a renewed effort at mobilization from above; it is, at the same time, an effort to respond to pressures from below, to adapt an increasingly anachronistic and ossified set of economic, political, and social institutions and norms to a changing society and a changing international environment.

Gorbachev's foreign policy strategy is a direct outgrowth of his domestic priorities. Economic and political reform is not only the key to domestic revitalization, in Gorbachev's view; it is essential to sustain the Soviet Union's international role. As Gorbachev himself described the linkage of his domestic and foreign policy program, the success of efforts at internal reform will determine whether or not the Soviet Union will enter the 21st century "in a manner worthy of a great power."

Not only is there an intimate connection between Gorbachev's domestic and foreign policies; there are striking parallels between the two. What they share is a demand for "new political thinking." They reflect a growing recognition within important segments of the Soviet elite that in a number of key areas previous policies have proven sterile and counterproductive, that they are ill-suited to the needs of the 1980s and beyond, and that a certain price must be paid to liquidate them. They both reflect as well a recognition that the rigidity and dogmatism of past practices have alienated potential sources of sympathy and support both domestically and internationally, depriving the Soviet model of any genuine appeal. And they reflect a determination to reorient Soviet domestic and foreign policies so as to associate the Soviet system with the real sources of dynamism in both the domestic and international arenas.

Gorbachev's reforms thus represent a movement toward the normalization of the Soviet system, a modification of some of the more aberrant features of Soviet domestic and foreign policy inherited from the Stalin era. They stem from a recognition that economic development and the growing maturity of Soviet society demand new approaches to its management.

Discussions of change in the Soviet Union all too often reject as without significance alterations which fall short of a fundamental structural transformation. Clearly, current developments do not fundamentally challenge the Party's monopoly of political power, or the key features of a command economy, or the state's monopoly over the critical channels of information and communication. Nor do they even approach the scale of changes currently under way in China. If our only criterion of significant change is the evolution of Communist systems toward market economies, liberal-democratic polities, and pluralist societies with independent bases of power, the current changes are insufficient to appear fundamental.

Yet, just as Khrushchev's reforms succeeded in dismantling several key features of the Stalinist system—the reliance on mass terror, the central role of the secret police, the untrammelled power of a dictatorial leader exalted in the cult of personality—and thereby significantly transformed the nature of Soviet politics, so too might Gorbachev's policies alter the way which the party/state deals with its own society. The broadening scope of quasi-autonomous economic, social, and cultural activity, and the retreat of the state from efforts to control it, may well herald the emergence of an embryonic civil society in Russia.

If Gorbachev's efforts are daunting in their scope, they are highly uncertain in their prospects. As recent developments in China—not to mention earlier experiences in Eastern Europe—should serve to remind us, the reform of Leninist systems is both difficult and reversible. The sheer technical complexity of the undertaking, the ideological and political challenge it poses, the bureaucratic resistance it inevitably engenders, and the popular conservatism and inertia it must overcome test the political skills and the will of even the most determined reformist leaders. Moreover, while previous attempts at reform in Eastern Europe were constrained by the threat of Soviet intervention, the Soviet leadership faces a constraint absent in Eastern Europe: the danger that reform will unleash centrifugal forces within the multinational Soviet system as well as threaten to destabilize its East European empire.

If Gorbachev's attempt at reform challenges deeply ingrained features of Soviet behavior, it also invites a reconsideration of some of our own assumptions about the nature of the Soviet system. In challenging the image of unchanging Communist systems, it raises fundamental questions about the potential scope as well as the limits of transformation—and, above all, about the linkage between domestic reform and international behavior. If it is indeed the case, as has often been argued, that the nature of the Soviet system itself is the source of its expansionist and aggressive foreign policy, then the process of normalization now under way creates the potential for far-reaching changes in East-West relations in the decades ahead.

This essay will explore three issues which are central to understanding current developments in the USSR and their implications for East-West relations: the sources of the impetus for change; Gorbachev's strategy for reform in both domestic and foreign policy; and the obstacles that strategy confronts, with a view to assessing both its long-term prospects and its implications for the West. It will then conclude with a discussion of the possible consequences for East-West relations of change in the Soviet Union.

THE SOURCES OF CHANGE

Gorbachev's strategy has its roots in a series of broad political and social changes that created both the context and the impetus for reform in the Soviet Union: the gradual erosion, which became increasingly visible by the late 1970s, of confidence in the Soviet regime within the broader society, and in Brezhnev's political leadership within the broader elite. This growing malaise and even alienation were the product of two mutually reinforcing trends: an objective deterioration in the performance of the Soviet economy, which brought in its wake a mounting array of social and political problems; and a growing mood of demoralization within the Soviet elite, reflecting a subtle but profound shift in perceptions of the regime's performance. Their effects were exacerbated further by the immobility of an aging political leadership unable to act effectively to reverse the decline.

The deteriorating performance of the Soviet economy was the critical catalyst in the growing perception of failure. For the first time since Stalin's death, slowing rates of economic growth made it impossible to guarantee, by the late 1970s, a simultaneous increase in per capita consumption, investment, and military spending. As the competition over increasingly scarce resources intensified, a growing gap between mass expectations of continued improvement in living standards and the leadership's capacity to satisfy them threatened the implicit "social compact" which had replaced the extensive reliance on mass terror and coercion and which had served as the cornerstone of stability in the post-Stalin era.

The economic slowdown was compounded by technological backwardness, creating yet a second "gap" of profound political and psychological importance: the gap which increasingly separated the Soviet economy from those of other advanced industrial societies, as well as from the dynamic newly-industrializing countries of Asia, from South Korea to Singapore. As a new industrial revolution transformed the international economy, placing a high premium on rapid technological innovation, speedy communication, and high-quality products, the Soviet system increasingly appeared to be relegated to marginality, a comparative backwater whose economic performance, increasingly incommensurate with its political ambitions, threatened to jeopardize its military prowess.

Economic slowdown and diminished international competitiveness coincided with and contributed to an increasingly negative assessment of the regime's performance, reflecting a change in the criteria used to evaluate it, a growing sense of failure, and growing pessimism about the future—in effect, a crisis of confidence within the Soviet elite. By the early 1980s not only Western observers but key Soviet officials were themselves, in a fashion unprecedented since the early 1920s, beginning to use the term "crisis" to convey the urgency of the situation.[2]

This dramatic shift in attitudes was rooted in broader social and demographic changes in the post-Stalin era, which transformed the passive and inarticulate peasant society of the Stalin era into an urban industrial society with an increasingly articulate and assertive middle class. The society over which Khrushchev presided in the 1950s was still predominantly rural. By the mid-1980s, in contrast, two thirds of the Soviet population lived in cities, and a growing share had been born in them. Moreover, the spread of television brought urban life styles and values to the remotest corners of Soviet territory. Even in 1965 fewer than one in three Soviet families owned television sets; by 1986 ownership was almost universal.

Rapid urbanization was accompanied by a dramatic rise in the educational attainments of the Soviet population. In 1959 two thirds of the Soviet population over the age of ten had no more than a primary education; by 1986 almost two thirds had completed secondary education. In 1959 only five and a half million Soviet citizens had higher education, compared to twenty-two million in 1986. The growth in the number of "scientific workers" was especially dramatic: from one and a half million in 1950 to fifteen million in 1986.[3]

In short, by the mid-1980s a large urban middle class, including a substantial professional, scientific-technical and cultural intelligentsia, had emerged as a major actor on the Soviet scene.

The attitudes and behaviors of this urban middle class sharply diverged from the conventional image of the "new Soviet man," and came to resemble in important respects those of its counterparts elsewhere. Whether in the burgeoning "second economy" or in a blossoming popular culture (facilitated by newly available technologies, from automobiles to VCRs, whose use is not readily amenable to central control), official norms and institutions were progressively supplanted by new forms of largely autonomous expression responsive to the preferences of consumers rather than officials.

The ability of the Soviet leadership to channel and shape the direction of social change has been strikingly diminished in the post-Stalin era. The image of "revolution from above," with all its connotations of state domination of a passive society, no longer corresponds to a reality where social forces have achieved a degree of autonomy and indeed actively impinge on the political system in unprecedented ways. The erosion of political control over important sectors of Soviet life is abundantly illustrated by the evolution of the "second economy," which by its very existence subverts centrally established priorities and challenges centralized control over prices, income distribution, and the allocations of capital and manpower. The spread of corruption, particularly within the political elite, threatens the organizational integrity and political legitimacy of the Party, and feeds both the resentment of those excluded from patronage and the hostility of those critical of its existence.

A parallel development is visible in the escape of important dimensions of social behavior from official control. People marry, reproduce, and divorce without reference to official demographic policy; they migrate from north and east to south and west, in defiance of planners' preferences; and their devotion to religious beliefs and practices resists all efforts to invigorate atheistic propaganda. A whole spectrum of social pathologies, from alcoholism and drug addiction to crime, dramatize the limits of political control.

This broader shift in values within the educated elite during the 1960s and 1970s, best captured in works of Soviet literature but visible as well in social science scholarship, centers on four broad themes. The first is a shift from the emphasis on party-mindedness (*partinost*) to preoccupation with universal moral concerns: the meaning of truth, the nature of good and evil, the moral significance of memory. The popularity of contemporary Soviet writers whose works address such themes, such as the Kirgiz novelist Chingiz Aitmatov, and the intense discussions they provoke in Soviet literary and cultural journals, are important indicators of the values and concerns of the educated public.

A second trend is a shift away from collectivism, with its image of a solitary society, to increased recognition of individual and social diversity and ultimately of the potential for social conflict. In scholarly writings on social stratification or on nationality issues, the scope and durability of class and ethnic differences is not merely acknowledged but legitimized, and—to borrow a metaphor from American social science—the vision of a Socialist future has been transformed from a melting pot to a salad bowl.

The open recognition of conflicting interests is a precondition of serious political discussion in any society, bearing as it does on the allocation of rewards. It is therefore of no small significance that two of the major intellectual debates of the 1970s and 1980s have centered on the nature of contradictions in socialist society and on the meaning of social justice.

Related to this trend away from collectivism was a shift from acceptance of the notion of a "single truth" to a recognition of the legitimacy and indeed the necessity of divergent opinions. While the post-Stalin era was marked by a considerable broadening of the boundaries of permitted discussion on a whole range of issues, the insistence that open discussion was a precondition of scientific progress as well as of cultural vitality, and should extend from technical to political issues, directly challenged the traditional claims of party ideology.

A fourth trend has been the gradual retreat from utopia and a growing relaxation of the limits of social engineering. Where social pathologies—from chauvinism to corruption, from drug addiction to crime—were once treated as "relics of the past," with the implicit assumption that a vast chasm would separate the socialist society of the future from its capitalist counterpart, current discussions of social problems accept their universality in all social systems, focus on how such behaviors are socially reproduced, and direct energies toward incremental improvements rather than eradication.

This impressionistic sketch of emergent attitudes and values by no means exhausts an increasingly rich, diverse, and complex spectrum of expression, not all of whose manifestations tended toward liberalization and increased tolerance. Side by side with this incipient reformism, and equally alienated from the ethos of the Brezhnev era, two other currents commanded some support in this urban milieu. One was a technocratic orientation that sought the solution to current problems in the application of new scientific and technological processes and products, and of managerial techniques, and saw in the military economy a possible model for emulation. The second was, if anything, antitechnological, identifying with a romantic nationalism that found its symbolism in the Russian past and protesting the ravages inflicted on nature and culture by the unbridled pursuit of industrialism and material progress.

The spiritual alienation of important segments of the intelligentsia would not have had so serious an impact, had it not become entwined with the deteriorating economic situation of the late 1970s. Detente further compounded the problem. By increasing the exposure of Soviet citizens to the outside world, it provided new criteria and reference groups for evaluating Soviet achievements and shortcomings. Judged by these standards, Soviet performance was increasingly found wanting, and previous official explanations of failure no longer seemed convincing. In the face of mounting domestic and international problems and the virtual paralysis of an aging and infirm leadership, the demoralization of an influential scientific-technical and cultural intelligentsia resentful of (and frustrated by) an authoritarian, patronizing, and exclusionary pattern of political rule constituted an important impetus for reform.

GORBACHEV'S STRATEGY

When he finally succeeded to power in 1985, Gorbachev

brought to the Soviet leadership no compelling vision of the future, nor a detailed blueprint for moving toward it. Neither a "true believer" like Khrushchev (who was disposed toward egalitarian, utopian and populist programs) nor a conservative bureaucrat like Brezhnev (who was concerned with protecting the status and privileges of fellow members of the elite), Gorbachev is the first modern Soviet leader, vastly more attuned than his predecessors to the imperatives of a scientific-technological age, pragmatic rather than ideological in his approach to problems, and concerned with rationalizing and making more efficient the system he had inherited.[4] He is confident of its basic stability and of its legitimacy in the eyes of the Soviet population, sharply critical of its performance, and impatient with the heavy weight of inherited dogma and bureaucratic inertia. But he has no ready answers as to how it should be improved.

Gorbachev came to power, moreover, as the head of a reform-oriented coalition, united in its critical assessment of past policies and performance and agreed on the need to move vigorously and decisively to break with the Brezhnevite past, but lacking a shared consensus on a strategy of reform or on its scope. The common denominator of the coalition was support for energetic leadership, greater discipline, a revival of the asceticism and civic virtue associated with the heroic periods of Soviet history, and a reassertion of effective control of the strategic levers of power by the center. Beyond this common core, however, it encompassed divergent views on how to move from discipline to revitalization, and varying degrees of willingness to sacrifice traditional forms of control for the sake of stimulating greater popular initiative.

The evident contradictions in the policies pursued over the past two years are thus in part a product of the very nature of the reform coalition and the different orientations within it. They are also a result of a process of learning. From the summer of 1986, Gorbachev's speeches reveal a growing realization that the problems he inherited were more complex, and the obstacles to reform more daunting, than he initially appreciated. They are marked by a perceptible radicalization, a gradual shift from an emphasis on "acceleration" (*uskorenie*) — a speeding up of the tempo within a basically stable framework — to a focus on "restructuring" (*perestroika*), which contemplates more radical and even fundamental change.

Gorbachev initially came to power with three rather traditional reformist priorities: to consolidate his political power; to arrest the deterioration of civic morale, restore discipline, and launch a process of social renewal; and to undertake economic reforms that would reverse the economic stagnation and technological backwardness of the Soviet economy and inject a dynamism now largely absent.

To this first task Gorbachev brought considerable personal assets, most notably his comparative youth, formidable energy, and consummate political skill. He also brought to the leadership a strong commitment to reform, shaped by his formative years as a law student at Moscow University during the early part of the Khrushchev era and by his continuing association with reform-minded intellectuals and professionals afterwards. He benefited from a psychological climate favorable to strong and decisive leadership — an understandable reaction to the long period of indecision and drift which characterized the succession of aging and infirm leaders — and from a demographic situation that gave him considerable opportunity to speed the retirement of an entire generation of leaders from the Party, state, military, and ministerial apparatuses and to fill an exceptionally large number of vacancies with his own appointees.

But he also came to power with some real liabilities: a limited political base of his own, particularly outside the Russian republic, and the presence of numerous well-entrenched regional leaders who had taken advantage of the stability and security afforded by Brezhnev's cadres policy to strengthen their own positions and build protective networks of informal ties based on patronage, nepotism, and corruption. Moreover, the evolution of the Soviet political system itself in the years since Stalin's death had eroded many of the bases of power and authority associated with Stalin's rule. Terror and violence were no longer available as political tools, nor was a reliance on personality cults; and even the personnel weapon had been weakened by expectations of security within the elite.

A second priority in Gorbachev's initial strategy was his campaign for social renewal. In a dramatic effort to arrest and reverse a widespread and snowballing atmosphere of decay, corruption, and cynicism, the new leadership sought to command the attention of the Soviet population and vigorously assert its authority with three highly visible campaigns—one directed against violations of work discipline, the second against alcoholism, and the third against corruption, particularly within the elite. These campaigns, moreover, would in the short term boost economic performance by increasing labor productivity and tapping unused reserves of labor and capital. The highly publicized attack on corrupt officials assured the working class that it was not the only target of renewed social discipline—and, simultaneously, provided the new leadership with a device for replacing political opponents.

Gorbachev's third priority was to carry out an economic reform to arrest the stagnation in growth rates and introduce a self-sustaining process of technological innovation that would create the essential foundation for superpower status. The urgent need to shift from an extensive to an intensive pattern of economic growth had long been recognized, but bureaucratic inertia and political resistance thwarted earlier, half-hearted attempts at reform under Brezhnev.

Gorbachev's strategy seeks simultaneously to strengthen central control over strategic planning decisions and to enhance initiative and responsibility at the enterprise level by striking at the middle levels of the stifling economic bureaucracy. It reflects a recognition that excessive insistence on control actually reduces the power of the center, and that relinquishing control over details may be essential to regaining leverage over key outcomes. Greater latitude for enterprise management will also entail increased responsibility, as profitability becomes the main criterion of performance and bankruptcy the penalty for failure. Workers as well as enterprises will face a more competitive environment if the economic reform proceeds. Increased wage differentials, and a reduction of job security, are an effort to enhance the rewards for initiative and productivity and impose more severe penalties for failure.

The proposed reforms also seek to encourage private initiative in agriculture and in the services—where centralized planning has proven least effective, where poor quality and limited availability of desired goods and services had been a perennial source of complaints, where dependence on supplies from other sectors is lower than in much of industry, and where the precedent of Lenin's Economic Policy of 1921 (explicitly invoked by Gorbachev) makes ideological constraints less inhibiting. The expansion of collective farm markets selling agricultural produce in urban areas, the spread of private or cooperative restaurants, the encouragement of cooperative housing construction, and the creation of a network of establishments providing needed consumer services are envisioned as a modest contribution to improving the living conditions of the Soviet population much as such measures have done in Hungary. The success of such initiatives, however, depends on the cooperation of local authorities, and complaints abound of their resistance to new proposals.

Finally, Gorbachev's economic strategy also involves new international economic policies which would rely on the limited use of joint ventures with capitalist firms and on greater involvement in international economic institutions to attract Western capital, technology, entrepreneurship, and managerial skills to Soviet enterprises. Moreover, by obliging joint ventures to produce for an international market as well as an internal one, economic policymakers are seeking to challenge Soviet enterprises to meet international standards of quality. Whether the terms proposed will elicit the desired Western response remains in question. What all these elements of economic reform have in common, however, is an increased reliance on the discipline of the marketplace to make the Soviet products more competitive and to challenge the sway of a "protectionism" that has long insulated the Soviet economy from outside influences and protected enterprises and workers from the consequences of failure.

But the novelty and significance of Gorbachev's strategy goes beyond the three initial concerns described so far. They lie in Gorbachev's recognition that Soviet society has reached a level of maturity that requires a new approach to its governance, that the Soviet people, and particularly the educated middle classes, could no longer be treated as the objects of official policy but had to be treated as genuine subjects. They express his growing realization, in short, that successful reform rests at bottom on redefining the relationship of state and society.

Khrushchev had launched the process of inclusion—a shift, however erratic, from the centralized, coercive statism of the Stalinist system to a more conciliatory and flexible approach to social forces. Gorbachev seeks to extend it further. His advocacy of *glasnost,* of cultural liberalization, and of "democratization" is not merely a tactical device to secure the support of the intelligentsia for his economic and political program or a public-relations effort aimed at world opinion. It reflects a profound recognition that an embryonic civil society has begun to emerge in the Soviet Union, and an unprecedented willingness to lend the process official encouragement.

The endorsement of *glasnost,* with its simultaneous connotation of both candor and publicity, stands at the center of this effort. It is, of course, a policy of preemption, intended to reduce the reliance of the Soviet population on foreign and unofficial sources of information—from foreign television and radio broadcasts to gossip—to fill the voids created by Soviet silence. *Glasnost* is also a symbol of trust. It reflects a recognition by the Soviet leadership of the maturity of the Soviet people, and a partial repudiation of the patronizing notion that only a small elite could be entrusted with truth. It marks a real break with the entire Bolshevik conception of a vanguard party, premised as it was on the need for tutelage over backward masses.

Glasnost is equally an expression of confidence in the basic legitimacy of the Soviet system, and in its leadership, a recognition that the pretense of infallibility is no longer necessary to command popular allegiance and support. Indeed, greater publicity for shortcomings and problems—whether the shoddy construction of nuclear power plants or the spread of drug addiction—is an indispensable precondition for successfully addressing them.

The case for *glasnost* and its intimate connection to the prospects for reform was most eloquently put by Tatiana Zaslavskaya, the reformist sociologist, who argued in a remarkable article in *Pravda:*

> If we continue to keep from the people information about
> the conditions under which they live, say the degree of envi-
> ronmental pollution, the number of industrial accidents, or the
> extent of crime, we cannot expect them to assume a more ac-
> tive role in economic or in political life. People will trust and
> support you only if you trust them.[5]

Finally, and of potential significance for the future, *glasnost* is linked to accountability. An expanded and more independent role for the media—including serious investigative reporting—is an important instrument for exposing abuses of power and position and for holding officials accountable for their actions. Needless to say, it also offers a convenient weapon for use against political opponents. It is nonetheless of great importance that *glasnost* has extended, in however tentative a manner, to the first ginger exposés of abuses by the police and the KGB. Even foreign policy and military affairs, largely exempted from public discussion, have begun to receive closer scrutiny; and Western journalists, scientists and congressmen have been given unprecedented access to several Soviet installations.

Glasnost extends to the treatment of the Soviet past as well as the present. The process of de-Stalinization, interrupted and partially reversed under Brezhnev, has regained momentum, and has provoked some of the sharpest public debates of the Gorbachev era. Two key cultural events—the publication of Anatoli Rybakov's *Children of the Arbat* and the screening of Tengiz Abuladze's *Repentance*—involve unprecedentedly frank and powerful evocations of the crimes of the Stalin era, with clear political ramifications. Gorbachev's endorsement of a fuller and more accurate version of earlier Soviet history has encouraged the publications of previously unpublished memoirs and documents which shed light on important and sensitive historical events, such as the forcible collectivization of agriculture, the assassination of

Sergei Kirov in 1934, and the Great Purges that followed. It has also invoked a reexamination of the alternatives to Stalin.

The Gorbachev era is also characterized by apparent official acceptance of a more differentiated conception of society. A progressive erosion of earlier emphases on solidarity, homogeneity, and uniformity has been accompanied by the emergence of a new orientation that, at the very highest level, recognizes a diversity of groups and interests, and the possibility of fundamental conflicts among them.

Indeed a transformation of Soviet ideology, if not its actual erosion, is itself under way, most visible in the dramatic change that the Party ideological journal *Kommunist* itself has undergone under editors appointed by Gorbachev. Lenin's conception of a single truth and an infallible approach to problems no longer holds sway; contributions present diverse and contradictory approaches to current problems and invite readers to join the discussion. The very introduction of formal debate on Soviet television, with its presentation of two diametrically opposed positions on major issues of the day without any final resolution—including the desirability of reform, or whether Gorbachev should go to Reykjavik—is a dramatic departure from longstanding behavior.

Gorbachev clearly aligned himself with the advocates of ideological change at the January 1987, Central Committee Plenum when he criticized what he called a "schematic and dogmatic approach" to Party ideology characteristic in the past. His speech echoed a striking article that had appeared in late 1986 in *Izvestia* calling for greater debate and controversy on major issues of the day. "We must get used to the idea that a multiplicity of voices is a natural part of openness," its author had argued.

> We must treat diversity normally, as the natural state of the world; not with clenched teeth, as in the past, but normally as

an immutable feature of social life . . . . We need in the economy and other areas of Soviet life a situation where multiple variants and alternative solutions are in and of themselves development tools and preconditions for obtaining optimal results, and where the coexistence of two opposing points of view on a single subject is most fruitful.[6]

All of these themes come together in the issue that has emerged as the most fundamental—and the most explosive—dimension of Gorbachev's strategy: his advocacy of democratization. Gorbachev appears to have concluded that the success of the entire reform effort ultimately depends on whether the Soviet people can be actively engaged in the process, and whether a greater sense of participation will at least partially compensate for the absence of other immediate payoffs. His campaign for democratization seeks to encourage more extensive involvement in grass-roots economic and political life, more candid discussions of problems in the workplace and in local state and party organizations, and greater accountability by leaders to the population as a whole.

Tentative discussions of legal reform also have important implications for political democratization. Measures that would curb the arbitrary interference of officials in judicial procedures, strengthen guarantees of "socialist legality," offer greater protection to defendants, and define more narrowly what constitutes "anti-Soviet behavior" would provide an essential foundation for creating a more genuine sense of citizenship. Gorbachev's decision to permit the return of Andrei Sakharov to Moscow, and his vigorous participation in public affairs, is an important milestone in this process.

Gorbachev's increasing focus on the need for democratization has brought to the forefront a fundamental tension that runs through virtually the entire reform effort: the tension between the urgent need to enhance initiative and the fear of losing control. Gorbachev addressed the deepest anxieties of the party apparatus when he acknowledged that "democracy without openness does not exist. But at the same time, democracy without a framework is anarchy. That is why it will be complex." [7]

Leninism from its inception was fearful of spontaneity and preoccupied with maximizing control. Faced with the urgent need for new approaches to managing a modern economy and society, Gorbachev has inherited an old dilemma and is casting about for a fresh approach to its resolution. By contrast with Khrushchev and Mao, who sought to mobilize popular initiative against the Party and bureaucratic apparatus, Gorbachev is trying to ensure greater accountability of leadership within existing institutions. Nonetheless, the potential for turbulence and conflict is very real.

The enormity of the challenge he has launched, and the limited support on which it is based, have compelled Gorbachev to seek new sources and instruments of leverage. In the effort to overcome the resistance and inertia of the Party and state bureaucracies and to mobilize broader support for his programs, Gorbachev has turned to the media as a major political resource. Indeed, one of the most intriguing features of the recent Soviet scene is the way in which the media have emerged as a novel and influential instrument of political power. Technological changes have created new tools of communication, most notably mass access to television, which has in a very short time rendered obsolete the entire agitprop system which was long the linchpin of Soviet political socialization. Indeed, Gorbachev is the first Soviet leader to appreciate fully and utilize this development. By placing supporters in key positions in ideological and cultural institutions—for example, as head of the ideological and cultural department within the Central Committee, or as the editors of influential journals—he has sought to shape the terms of the debate over reform to his political advantage and to compensate for his relative weakness in the more traditional organs of power.

NEW DEPARTURES IN FOREIGN POLICY

In foreign as in domestic policy, Gorbachev's succession has prompted a serious reassessment of previous assumptions and policies, and has brought with it dramatic departures in virtually every aspect of Soviet relations with the outside world.

Gorbachev's foreign policy, as he himself has argued on several occasions, is a direct outgrowth of his domestic priorities. Indeed, the two are more closely entwined at this juncture than at any previous time in postwar Soviet history. Economic reform is not only the key to domestic revitalization, in Gorbachev's view; it is essential to sustain the Soviet Union's international role. To gain the time necessary to consolidate his power and carry out his domestic programs, Gorbachev urgently needs both a respite from external pressures and evidence of external success. He has therefore centered his efforts on shaping an international environment that will be more hospitable to domestic reform, and a foreign policy that gives increased recognition to nonmilitary dimensions of security.

Gorbachev's approach has three key features. The first is his effort to revive the atrophied instruments of Soviet diplomacy to project a more positive and dynamic Soviet image abroad, to convey an image of moderation and good-neighborliness and of willingness to seek political settlements to outstanding issues, while reducing the costs and risks of Soviet involvements in the international arena. The second is to extricate the Soviet Union from dead-end positions, including the excessive preoccupation with military power, wherever this can be accomplished without fundamentally threatening

149

Soviet geostrategic interests and alliance systems. Finally, Gorbachev urgently needs to generate the resources for urgent domestic economic needs, both by sharply cutting military expenditures and by attracting Western capital and technology, in part through joint ventures.

Gorbachev's initial strategy has focused above all on an effort to reduce tensions simultaneously with the United States and China and to reap the domestic economic political benefits of that achievement. His willingness to consider far-reaching arms control, intrusive verification, and unilateral cutbacks rests on the recognition that the military buildup and confrontational foreign policy pursued by his predecessors not only failed to enhance Soviet security but may have endangered it by provoking military countermeasures and greater political coordination in both Western Europe and Asia.

The United States remains the central, if less exclusive, Soviet preoccupation, and arms control its primary focus. Soviet policy in the past three years has been marked by new initiatives across the entire range of arms-control negotiations, as well as by an unprecedented willingness to address the thorny problem of verification. The signing of an INF agreement and progress in talks on strategic-arms limitations as well as conventional forces have been facilitated by major Soviet concessions.

Apparent, though still ambiguous, shifts in Soviet doctrine toward an emphasis on military "sufficiency" rather than "parity," and on a "non-offensive defense," are intended both to reassure the NATO alliance about Soviet intentions and to reduce internal pressures to "keep up with the United States" in defense expenditures. In an effort to blunt possible political challenges, Gorbachev has portrayed advocates of stepped-up military spending as playing into the hands of Western "hawks," and has emphasized the shared interests and interdependence of East and West rather than focusing on competition and confrontation. Soviet policy under Gorbachev has also demonstrated an exceptionally subtle appreciation of the domestic forces affecting American foreign policy, whether in its recognition that extreme Soviet secretiveness helped feed Western mistrust and fear of Soviet intentions, or in its readiness to modify some of the more odious previous practices concerning human rights and Jewish emigration. The return of Andrei Sakharov from exile, and the release of a number of prominent dissidents and refuseniks, were important gestures in this effort, as was the decision to allow a group of American scientists to monitor Soviet underground tests, or a Congressional delegation to visit the controversial Krasnoyarsk radar.

The improvement of Soviet relations with China, which had taken its first halting steps under Brezhnev in 1983, was similarly given new impetus by Gorbachev's accession to power. Gorbachev's own commitment to reform contributed to a more positive view of developments in China than had previously prevailed within the Soviet leadership—and an acknowledgment that, like the Soviet Union, China was engaged in an effort to build "a socialist society worthy of a great people." [8]

The gradual economic and political rapprochement, as well as new Soviet policies which addressed Chinese concerns—withdrawing from Afghanistan, reducing troops along the borders, and pressing for a political settlement in Cambodia—paved the way for a Sino-Soviet summit to take place this spring. Indeed, greater tolerance for diversity within the socialist community more generally has been a hallmark of the Gorbachev era.

These and other Soviet initiatives around the globe constitute a concerted and ambitious effort to overcome the political isolation and economic marginality of Moscow in the early 1980s; to regain the diplomatic initiative; to win breathing space for domestic revitalization; and to make the Soviet Union a more constructive member of the international community. Should they continue, they present the West with unprecedented opportunities for reshaping the global agenda in the years ahead.

THE PROSPECTS

Gorbachev's reforms have already brought important changes to the Soviet system, but they are by no means irreversible. Indeed, all the evidence suggests that Gorbachev is pursuing a high-risk strategy which confronts significant obstacles to success.

Although significant policy changes across a wide range of areas are already evident, most notably in Soviet culture, as these changes increasingly impinge on core institutional arrangements the obstacles, and the resistance, mount. This is especially true of efforts at economic reform, where key features of the Soviet economy are not only closely intermeshed but tightly bound to the nature of the Soviet political system and ultimately to the role of the Party itself. To shift from the administrative allocation of resources to an increased reliance on market mechanisms is ultimately to challenge the very *raison d'être* of the Party, in the USSR as in China.

Second, reform is not only a technical process but a highly political one, involving fundamental changes in the allocation of resources, status, and power in the Soviet system. It has already brought latent and long-repressed conflicts of interest to the surface, and is likely to trigger further manifestations of working-class, and especially of ethnic, grievances. Cultural liberalization, political democratization, and *glasnost* are a potent recipe for ever greater expression of grievance and for unprecedented manifestations of social, political, and international conflict in a system long unaccustomed to dealing with them openly and lacking the mechanisms for resolving rather than repressing conflict. Managing these conflicts effectively will pose a major political challenge.

A third source of resistance lies in the bureaucracy itself, a largely passive resistance of established routines, of inertia, but one which has demonstrated a formidable capacity over the years to absorb and domesticate reforms rather than be transformed by them.

Beyond passive resistance, Gorbachev confronts outright political opposition, not yet highly visible, not yet organized, and without as yet an alternative program of its own, but an opposition that draws sustenance from the widespread anxiety which these changes have already provoked by blurring familiar boundaries, eroding stable expectations, and bringing long-repressed conflicts to public attention. Abundant evidence is available, if any is needed, of bitter antagonism to many of Gorbachev's initiatives, from the release of prominent dissidents, to what is perceived as a surfeit of *glasnost,* from an excessively critical assessment of the Stalin era to the attack on elite privileges, from the potential challenge of democratization to the very role of the *nomenclatura.* Opposition to Gorbachev's initiatives in foreign and security policy, while less visible, is equally real, and it is far from certain whether they would outlast his removal from power.

Finally, Eastern Europe constitutes a significant constraint on the prospects for reform in the Soviet Union. The irony of Gorbachev's triumphal visit to Prague—accompanied by the Czech party leader who owed his position to the defeat of Alexander Dubcek—was hardly lost on Eastern Europe. Gorbachev and his colleagues have learned the lessons of 1968, and they may well be determined that instability in Eastern Europe will never again be permitted to halt the reform of the Soviet system. But the situation is inherently unstable, and a serious eruption in Eastern Europe is bound to reverberate in Moscow.

Gorbachev's reforms seek to tap the sources of vitality and dynamism that have increasingly developed outside the Soviet system, to draw back into the official economy, policy, and culture individuals and activities that had deserted it or been excluded. Whether or not his reforms will prove successful, and indeed how to measure success, remains an open question. Gorbachev has posed the issue sharply: "There is nowhere to retreat to." [9]

"Either democratization or social inertia and conservatism," he has said. "There is no third way." [10]

History, however, may afford less stark choices.

State of the World, 2000: What We Should Do to Affect It

Peter H. Raven

With a dozen short years separating us from the end of the century, most of us continue to act as if only the immediate future matters. We tend to view changes in the environment—the water, soils, air, plants, and animals on which we base all of our activities and every bit of our prosperity—as if they would simply always be there. Major trends "happen to us," and we hope that perhaps the future will somehow take care of itself. Meanwhile, our rapidly growing numbers are relentlessly and in some cases permanently exacting a toll on the ability of the earth to support us. In our preparation for the year 2000 and beyond, we must find the ways to reverse some of the more threatening trends that confront us.

It is the opinion of many observers, including myself, that if we do not find the way to deal with some of these trends, the human race is unlikely to be able to continue its progress into the future; the 21st century will be very much poorer, with many fewer opportunities and many more threats, than the twentieth.

The lights that are visible from satellites or night flights almost anywhere on earth, the large-scale changes in the composition of the atmosphere that we are causing, the die-off of trees throughout much of the world because of industrial pollution, the very fact that there is no longer a square inch anywhere on earth in which chemical pollutants do not fall—all

155

of these relationships signal us of our huge and growing impact on the productive capacity of the earth. As we consider the ways in which we can intelligently utilize our earth in the future, let us remember that a rapidly growing fraction of the world's population is now poor. To increase their standard of living implies an increasingly intensive use of the available food, energy, and other goods available on earth—a process made more urgent by future population increases.

In the following pages, I shall first outline some of these trends briefly, and then move on to discuss some appropriate ways in which we can address them if we find the will to do so.

POPULATION PRESSURE

About five million people populated the entire world eleven thousand years ago, when agriculture was first developed in several widely separated centers. The ability to cultivate plants and animals for our use allowed people to live together in more or less permanent settlements; in these towns, the specialization of skills occurred, and the beginnings of what we know as civilization began to appear. Far fewer people than now inhabit greater Chicago were spread over all of Eurasia and Africa, and some of them were about to enter the New World for the first time. In addition, the stage was set for the progressive, worldwide reduction in biological diversity that has continued up to the present.

By the time of Christ, the global population amounted to some one hundred and forty million people. We reached the level of one billion people only about three hundred years ago, and the subsequent rate of growth of our population has been truly staggering, a point that cannot be overstressed. Another way of making the same point is to indicate that the global population has doubled since 1950, a date that seems very recent to most of us; the century began with about 1.6 billion people, and it will end with more than six billion!

When will the world population stabilize? According to "medium" United Nations estimates, this may occur at a level of about ten billion people in the next century, although other estimates project that our numbers will continue to grow for another century beyond that. The UN estimate depends on the assumption that women worldwide will average about two children each by 2035. If the average number of children per mother is actually higher, the number of people in 2050 or 2100 could be much greater than ten billion. Such estimates also depend on steadily increasing life expectancies, with improved health and sanitation measures being implemented. At present, the global population is growing at 1.7 percent per year, which amounts to an additional eighty-five million people—the equivalent of another Mexico—annually. If present rates of growth were sustained—and few think that they could be—the global population would double in just forty years, by the year 2028.

POVERTY

For convenience in our discussion, we can divide the distribution of people around the world into three major blocks: (1) the industrialized world; (2) China; and (3) the developing world. In 1950, when the global population was less than half of its present level, a third of the people in the world lived in industrialized nations. At present, the proportion is less than a quarter. By the early decades of the next century, it will be a sixth. The developing countries, most of which lie at least partly in the tropics or subtropics, were home to about 45 percent of the world's people in 1950. Today, 55 percent live there, and by the early years of the next century the figure will be approximately two thirds. In actual numbers, the 1.1

billion people who inhabited these countries thirty-eight years ago will quadruple to about five billion people within the next few decades—as soon as 2020, if present trends continue.

Even though most tropical countries have official population policies, the fact that an average of 40 percent of their people are less than fifteen years old—yet to reach the age at which they would normally be expected to have children—means that their populations will continue to grow for at least two or three more generations. In industrialized nations, only about 22 percent of the people are less than fifteen years old, so that their populations are growing much more slowly. For these reasons, the populations of developing countries will continue to grow much more rapidly than those of industrialized countries for at least several decades. The differences between the standards of living that are possible in these two groups of countries are likely to increase; for this reason alone, it is difficult to envision significant gains in standards of living for the people of tropical countries.

Regional differences can be measured in many different ways. The per capita GNP in industrialized countries is approximately $10,000, while that in less developed countries is about $660. Putting it another way, the 25 percent of us who live in industrialized countries base our standard of living on more than 82 percent of the world's wealth, whereas the rapidly increasing 75 percent of the people who live in the rest of the world enjoy the benefits of less than 18 percent of the total world economy. Many similar comparisons reveal similar ratios: For example, the use of industrial energy or minerals by the industrialized world amounts to 90 percent of the total available for most commodities. Furthermore, per capita income is declining both in Africa and Latin America, regions that are suffering depressions at least equivalent in intensity and general feeling of hopelessness to the Great Depression of the 1930s: Commodities are becoming less, rather than more, available to most of the world's people.

Within the developing world itself, the gap between rich and poor is very great, and it is increasing. Some 40 percent of the 2.7 billion people who live in tropical or subtropical regions outside of China live in a condition that the World Bank defines as absolute poverty. These people are unable to count on obtaining adequate food, shelter, and clothing from one day to the next. Of these, approximately two thirds eat fewer than 90 percent of the calories deemed necessary to lead an "active working life," and 300 to 400 million people consume less that 80 percent of this standard—a diet that typically stunts growth and leads to serious health risks. In addition, UNICEF has estimated that more than 14 million children under the age of five starve to death or die of disease unnecessarily each year in tropical and subtropical countries, amounting to 40,000 young children each day.

In addition to the millions of babies and young children who starve to death each year, many millions of additional children exist only in a state of lethargy, their mental capacities often permanently impaired by their lack of access to adequate amounts of food. Largely because of these relationships, the life expectancy at birth in sub-Saharan Africa is, at less than fifty years, about a third less than that in the United States or Western Europe.

MANAGEMENT OF THE BIOSPHERE

The rapidly growing global human population is a dominant ecological force, without precedent in the world's history. We, like all other organisms, depend on energy that is ultimately derived from the sun. Plants, algae, and a few kinds of bacteria have the ability to capture some of this energy, which bombards the earth continuously, and to incorporate it into molecules that supply the needs of all living things on earth. One of the obvious ways of measuring human dominance—remembering that we are one of no fewer than five million species on earth—is to calculate the proportion of the total energy available that we appropriate for ourselves. What fraction of the total do we consume directly, waste, or co-opt (as in clearing pastures)?

In the middle 1980s, the proportion of total global productivity that the industrialized nations appropriate was estimated at an alarming 40 percent of the amount available. Peter Vitousek and his colleagues at Stanford University calculated that people use this proportion of the total available material either directly or indirectly: Either it flows to consumers and decomposers other than it normally would (for example, in managed systems such as pastures), or it is lost because of human-caused changes in land use (in the conversions of forest into pasture, for example, or in desertification).

If we achieve no improvements in the ways in which we use the world's resources, we would need 80 percent of the total by the middle of the next century just to stay even—and that would imply that our use was sustainable, a proposition that we shall examine in more detail below.

At the same time, our industrial activities are rapidly changing the composition of our atmosphere. The global consumption of fossil fuels continues to rise, and trends in energy use are at the root of some of our most difficult environmental problems. The fourfold growth in the world's economy that occurred between 1950 and 1979 roughly paralleled the growth in use of fossil fuel, and has been accompanied by rapidly increasing concentrations of carbon dioxide (which has increased 25 percent in the atmosphere since 1900) and other gases.

As a result of these trends, the world climate is expected to rise between 1.5 and 4.5 degrees centigrade between now and 2050—a level of change that would cause catastrophic disruption to world agriculture—while the sea level may rise between 1.4 meters and 2.2 meters by 2100. Although alternative explanations are possible, the year 1987 was the warmest in recent history, and many scientists believe that the warming trend associated with atmospheric changes has already become evident.

More locally, some twenty-five hundred toxic sites in the United States alone urgently require clean-up. Acid precipitation and other forms of air pollution have damaged some twelve thousand square miles of temperate forest, amounting to a fifth of the total forested area in Europe, for example, and is seeping into the ground water, along with various toxic substances, in many areas. In regions such as the Middle East, serious water shortages and contamination by the year 2000 could bring upheaval throughout this politically volatile region.

THE TROPICS: CRITICAL AREA FOR
THE GLOBAL FUTURE

The problems we have been discussing are particularly acute in the tropics, where population growth is most rapid, human suffering most extensive, and the remedies for widespread poverty and starvation the most obscure. The fact is that we do not know much about replacing most tropical forests with productive agriculture and forestry. For many tropical soils, the combination of inefficient or short-term exploitation with disorganized logging and clearing, often by the poor, results in a long-term destruction of their potential productivity. As populations grow rapidly and become increasingly poor, methods that were suitable when human populations existed at lower levels and the forests had time to recover from temporary disturbances simply do not work any longer.

Clearing the woods or prairies of Eurasia or North America traditionally has led to the establishment of productive farms; clearing the forests of tropical Africa or Latin America often creates wastelands. The relative infertility of many tropical soils, their thin and easily disturbed surface layer of organic matter, and the high temperature and precipitation levels characteristic of tropical regions often combine to make sustainable agriculture or forestry impossible, at least with the techniques that are usually applied.

Tropical forests not only are being cleared and destroyed rapidly because of the needs of the people who live in or near them, but also because of the demands of the global economy. Many products—foods such as beef, bananas, coffee, tea, medicines, and hardwoods—come to the industrialized world from the tropics. As timber is harvested in the tropics, only a very limited amount of replanting is taking place: It is estimated that only one tree is planted for every ten cut in the tropics generally, and in Africa the proportion is much lower. The developed-world consumption of tropical hardwoods has risen fifteen times since 1950, while in-country consumption has increased only three times.

In global climatic terms, deforestation also contributes to increases in atmospheric carbon dioxide—the proportion of this gas in the atmosphere has risen by 30 percent since 1860—and thus to a steadily rising world temperature. The large-scale cutting of forests likewise is impairing the capacities of some tropical systems to recycle rainfall inland. In the Amazon, for example, where more than half of the precipitation is recycled, continued deforestation is likely to lead to increased erosion and water runoff, together with reduced evapotranspiration and ultimately reduced precipitation. Reduced precipitation in the Amazon could severely affect the climate and agriculture in south-central Brazil, and similar effects may already have contributed to the droughts of recent years in Africa.

Against this background, the recent inauguration of the International Tropical Timber Agreement as well as the organization of the Tropical Forest Action Plan by the World Resource Institute (WRI) are of great importance for the stable management of the world's resources. Even more significant is the agreement on ozone depletion, developed under the auspices of the United Nations Environment Program (UNEP) and signed in late 1987. Such international agreements clearly afford us one of the few opportunities we have to alleviate global environmental problems.

Meanwhile, however, tropical forests are being cleared and severely disturbed very rapidly. Lowland moist forests, or rain forests—biologically the richest areas on earth, and also the most fragile ecologically—have already been reduced to less than half of their original area. Today, the remaining forests constitute an area about two thirds the size of the continental United States, and they are being destroyed at such a rate that most will be gone within twenty-five or thirty years. Some of the most extensive forests in the Amazon Basin may last until the middle of the next century, but, in general, such forests will definitely soon be gone—unless there are major and immediate changes in global interrelationships that do not seem likely. Both the global economy and the activities of rural farmers are driving the destruction, and neither seems likely to change soon. Outside of the rain forests, other types of tropical forests, most of them seasonally dry, are being destroyed even more rapidly, and often consist only of fragments even at the present time.

One major factor in the progressive degradation of areas that have been cleared is the relentless search for firewood by the roughly 1.5 billion people who depend on it as their major source of fuel. The demand greatly exceeds the supply; in

India, for example, where forests could sustain an annual harvest of only thirty-nine million tons of wood, the annual demand is for one hundred and thirty-three million tons. As fuelwood prices rise sharply, its use is being increasingly restricted to relatively affluent people, thus denying the poor in many regions the ability to cook their food. Diseases that were once thought to be under control, because the microbes that cause them are killed by heat, are increasing again in regions such as northern India, and prospects for the future seem grim.

GLOBAL INTERRELATIONSHIPS

In industrialized countries such as the United States, we tend to think of tropical countries as competitors, potential markets, debtors, drug producers, and sources of illegal immigrants—politically unstable, often corrupt, and, in general, a problem. We do not spend much time thinking about the common stake we have in the management of the global ecosystem, or the ways in which we depend on one another. Generally speaking, what we would like developing countries to do is repay their debt; refrain from sending us exports that might compete with our own products; accept whatever exports we want to send to them in large quantities; not send us immigrants; and achieve political stability. Even though their populations are growing by some eighty million people a year, we like to imagine that they will improve their standards of living and somehow fit into a prosperous global economy.

One still hears that we should not assist developing countries in food production, because by doing so we injure our own possibilities for marketing our farm surpluses. Nothing could be more ridiculous: Starving nations do not constitute good markets for anything. The intensity of agricultural production in the United States is already so great that the potential for damage to resources and to the environment remains serious. In 1986, U.S. government outlays for farm support programs ($25.5 billion) were roughly equal to the total value of agricultural exports ($26.5 billion), a relationship that clearly is not promising for future expansion, or "feeding the world." Some 40 percent of American farmland produces for export, yet we have done little to understand our markets or to respond to their needs, much less to contribute to the stable and orderly sustainable development of the countries that purchase these exports.

These days, the international debt is a source of great worry for everyone. Certainly, its existence clearly encourages many Third World countries to overexploit their natural resources, without the creation of stable, productive alternatives: Logging restrictions are eased, poor farmers are displaced to regions that will not support them in the long term, the production of foods that the people can eat is decreased in favor of the production of export crops, and the associated austerity measures can throw large numbers of people out of work, thus increasing the extent of poverty in the nations involved. Although we in the United States are concerned about the stability of our banking system, what we should be even more concerned about is the stability of the global ecosystem and the potential of debt repayment for destabilizing the countries involved. Regardless of the legitimacy of the debt, Willy Brandt's characterization of efforts to repay it as "a blood transfusion from the sick to the healthy" come close to the mark. The runaway inflation associated with the debt in countries such as Brazil and Mexico has destabilized them still further, and helped to drive them deeper into depression. The rise of terrorism in Colombia and other countries further marks the failure of international cooperation to promote stability and promises even more trouble for the future.

Another familiar example of linkages is provided by the massive immigration of poor people from the tropics and subtropics into the industrialized nations of the temperate zone. The U.S. Immigration and Naturalization Service estimates that approximately 1.8 million aliens were apprehended at the Mexican border alone in 1986, suggesting that perhaps twice that many might have entered successfully. Even the dispossessed middle class in Mexico is joining the exodus in large numbers. The Census Bureau estimates that net immigration now accounts for 28 percent of population growth in the United States, and will account for all growth by the 2030s if present trends continue. In some sense, immigration from Third World countries to industrialized ones is a special case of the problem of refugees worldwide, which has assumed fundamental importance in many parts of the world. In February 1985, for example, the United Nations estimated that more than ten million Africans had left their homes in search of food, often crossing national borders in the process.

A final problem of linkages that should be mentioned concerns political instability in the tropics and subtropics and its effect on the industrial nations. The United States, the richest nation on earth and therefore the one with the most to lose from global instability, invests the lowest amount on a per capita basis in international development assistance of any industrialized nation. The erosion of U.S influence in Latin America has been rapid during the 1980s. Both our obsession with Nicaragua and our unwillingness to negotiate seriously about the debt issue have contributed to the decline of our regional influence.

True stability in developing countries will involve the incorporation of poor people into the economies of their regions, as well as the management of natural resources in such a way that they will continue to be productive in the long term. It can be achieved in no other way; and it cannot be achieved, during the next century at least, without the cooperation of industrialized nations.

BIOLOGICAL EXTINCTION:
THE LOSS OF OPPORTUNITY

We base our livelihood directly or indirectly on our ability to utilize plants, animals, and microorganisms, so that extinction of a large number of them poses a major problem for us. Much of the problem of extinction centers in the tropics, where at least two thirds of the species of plants, animals, and microorganisms exist, and where the ecosystems in which they live are being destroyed most rapidly. The proportions of species of well-known groups of organisms, such as plants and vertebrates, allows us to calculate that no fewer than 3 million species of tropical organisms exist, although there may be several times that many. The great majority of these are very poorly known. More than two thirds of these tropical organisms, constituting at least half of the total biological diversity in the world, occur only in and near forests that are being decimated over the next twenty-five or thirty years. Since most of them have highly specific ecological requirements, we can assume that many will not be able to exist under the radically different conditions that will arise as the forest is disturbed. For example, sun and wind will reach organisms formerly protected deep within the forest, and the very particular temperatures and humidities they may require for survival will not occur. In addition, when organisms occur in small pockets of vegetation, they occur in low numbers and become subject to extinction by chance alone. They also become inbred and may be genetically weakened. People hunt for them more intensively than before, because they are easier to find in the remaining small patches of vegetation than in the original forest; increasing numbers of people are also hunting fewer animals. Finally, if the regional climate changes as a result of clearing most of the forest, their small populations will be even more susceptible to extinction.

In general, a tenfold increase in area is necessary for a doubling in the number of species: For example, an island ten times the size of another in the same climatic zone will, on average, have twice as many species. This relationship allows us to calculate that a tenfold reduction in forest area will put half of the species that occurred at risk of extinction. In places such as Madagascar, western Ecuador, and the Atlantic coast forests of Brazil, this would appear already to have happened. Over the next twenty-five years or so, therefore, at least two million species, and probably many more, would seem to be in danger of extinction—and the great majority of them will be mostly or completely unknown when they disappear. If half of these actually do become extinct, the total will amount to more than a million species—over a fifth of the total number of species of plants, animals, and microorganisms in the world.

By the second half of the 21st century, many more species will become extinct unless steps are taken to preserve them; the remaining tropical forests will soon fall to the kinds of pressures that have been outlined above. Over the next thirty years, however, we can expect the rate of extinction to average more than a hundred species a day, with the rate increasing from perhaps a few species a day now to several hundred by the early years of the next century. The great majority of these species will be very poorly known, but clearly human potential will be permanently limited by their loss.

To find another episode of extinction like the present one, we would have to go back to the close of the Cretaceous Period, some 65 million years ago, when about two thirds of the species of terrestrial organisms disappeared. In the intervening time, there has been no rate of extinction even approaching one one-hundredth of the present level. Moreover, the total number of species in existence now is much greater than any that existed in the past, so the total numbers disappearing are far greater today.

As we have mentioned, industrialized nations derive many material benefits even now from the biological resources of the tropics, since they have the greatest technological capacity to exploit these properties and to afford them. For example, oral contraceptives for many years were produced from Mexican yams; muscle relaxants used in surgery worldwide come from an Amazonian vine; and the gene pool of corn has recently been enriched by the finding, on a small area in the mountains of Jalisco, Mexico, of a perennial wild relative.

We currently use only about 150 of the 250,000 kinds of plants as crops, but experts estimate that there are probably tens of thousands of additional ones that could produce food and other useful products. Many of these might be especially useful in the tropics, where the need is greatest. Unfortunately, we are likely to lose as many as 60,000 or so of the total number of plant species over the next two or three decades, simply by neglecting the fact that we are allowing them to disappear, thus cutting back our potential for the future by a quarter. In addition to their use as food, many plants offer other extraordinary possibilities as sources of medicines, oils, waxes, fibers, and other commodities of interest to our modern industrial society.

Genetic engineering affords us additional possibilities for the transfer of genes from one kind of organism to another, even though the donor may itself be of no economic interest whatever; indeed, as our techniques become more sophisticated, we shall come to depend even more heavily on biological diversity than we do now. In this sense, the availability of biotechnology affords an additional argument for the preservation of biological diversity, each species of plant or animal having tens of thousands of individual genes.

Finally, the uses of plants and algae as sources of biomass, and therefore of energy, should be mentioned. The sun is the ultimate source of clean, abundant energy, and plants and algae are probably the most efficient means of using it. As the temporary illusion of unlimited energy from fossil fuel comes to an end, biomass will be investigated intensively, and selections of plants and algae to grow under certain specific conditions will be made. For tropical countries, which are often energy-poor, biomass-producing or direct solar converters are especially attractive.

WHAT SHOULD BE DONE?

Simply stated, the explosive and unevenly distributed growth of a record human population is putting unsupportable strains on the carrying capacity of the global ecosystem. Many of us believe that only global understanding, and a mechanism whereby all people can work together for our common good, is the solution; but that is precisely the model that the founders of the United Nations had in mind when they came together in San Francisco in 1945, and our progress since then has not been very encouraging, to say the least. There are, however, a number of areas that seem to afford appropriate fields of concentration for us as we approach the year 2000, and I shall now discuss some of these.

Internationalism

One of the key steps in any rational approach to world problems is to promote internationalism—a common understanding that all of our human problems are interconnected. From the vantage point of a country such as the United States, attaining this objective is more difficult than it sounds; like most people everywhere, we tend to operate as if we were alone.

Even at the basic level of geographical literacy, our deficiencies are many, as demonstrated recently by the efforts of the National Geographic Society to assess geographical literacy in America. Americans are becoming more isolated from the rest of the world just when their dependency is being most clearly generated.

Yet American businesses depend on exports for 30 percent of their profits. Consider the possibilities for improving relationships, for example, between the United States and Latin America. As industrialized countries, the United States and Canada comprise 270 million people, their populations growing at 0.7 percent per year, with an average per capita income of $16,150 (1987). The developing countries of Latin America comprise 421 million people, their populations growing at 2.2 percent per year, with a per capita income of $1,700. By early in the next century, there will be twice as many people in Latin America as in the United States and Canada.

It is very much in the medium- and long-term interests of the United States and Canada to encourage the growing cooperation that exists among the nations of Latin America, and their efforts to help themselves. Positive political and economic developments should be encouraged, and development funds should be made available. When the United States deals with its neighbor Mexico, the primary issues discussed tend to be confrontational ones, emphasizing drug trafficking, illegal immigration, debt repayment, protective trade practices, and respective national policies toward the Central American conflict. Why could we not begin to move the agenda toward cooperative initiatives in science, technology, and the humanities; toward sustainable development and conservation; and toward mutual cultural understanding?

Would a deep and mutually considerate discussion of subjects of this sort not help to prepare us better for the increasingly intense interactions that will characterize our relationships in the next century?

Global Financial Interrelationships

In 1987, the international debt grew by 6.25 percent, to $1.19 trillion. In reporting this result, World Bank officials pointed out that such growth means "the relapse into poverty of large sections of the population." Since 1980, the debt burden has compressed personal incomes by about one seventh in middle-income developing countries, and by a quarter in the poorer countries. Increasing social and economic problems have appeared, and world economic growth has slowed appreciably. The U.S. trade deficit has increased as the ability of debtor countries to accept exports has worsened. Inflation is raging in the three biggest debtor countries, Brazil, Argentina, and Mexico, and domestic recovery programs are faltering everywhere.

Since 1985, neither the World Bank nor the International Monetary Fund has actually been able to make a net financial contribution to the Third World: Resources are being transferred from the developing countries to these agencies. Increasing skepticism by the wealthy countries that provide the basic funds for such activities is making it very difficult for them to reverse the flow.

The long-term problem with these relationships is apparent: The disorderly consumption of natural resources throughout most of the world is crippling their sustainability and threatening ever more severe cycles of starvation, political unrest, and economic instability in the future. It is directly in the interest of wealthy, industrialized nations to attempt to reverse the net flow of resources from poor to wealthy nations, and thus to construct political, economic, and ecological stability for the future. Direct development assistance, especially assistance targeted to the very poor, is of fundamental importance in the process. The evidence, however, suggests that few take these relationships seriously, preferring to undertake expensive and destructive military or economic manipulation after a particular situation has gone beyond repair, rather than to attempt to achieve results of lasting value first.

A Common Global Future

Wealthy countries such as the United States must use their assets to contribute disproportionately to the development of our common global future. Ways must be found to ameliorate the effect of the international debt in draining resources from the poor and transferring them to the rich. Meaningful development assistance must be provided by rich nations to poor nations, and they must be focused on the poor people of the countries that receive the assistance. Only in this way can stability be achieved. Such assistance should not be provided as charity but rather because of our shared obligation to use the world's resources wisely: to provide for the future.

The privileged status of the industrialized nations has allowed them to build up institutions and groups of trained people that go far beyond those existing in developing countries. For example, some 94 percent of the world's scientists live in industrialized countries, while only about 6 percent live in developing countries. Considering that developing countries also are home to about 75 percent of the world's population—increasing explosively and depleting natural resources in environmental conditions that are often poorly understood—the need becomes evident for full utilization of the intellectual capital of the industrial world for the common good.

Strenuous efforts must be made to create and to fund centers, networks (such as the African Academy of Sciences), and other institutions in which the need to develop science and technology for the Third World can be fostered effectively. Third World countries spend less than 0.2 percent of their GNP on science and technology, while industrialized nations spend 2.0 to 2.5 percent. They both expend about 5.6 percent on defense. With differences of this magnitude, the gap between the two groups of nations regarding the availability of science and technology becomes wider and wider.

In the context of the global effort that will be necessary, however, it also becomes evident that the United States and other industrialized nations cannot afford to waste the potential for contribution of any of their citizens. Women and minorities must be given every opportunity to contribute fully to the progress of society. This is true whether one is thinking of "international competitiveness" and other aspects of promoting the interests of the industrialized countries themselves, or whether one is thinking in terms of their obligation (and self-interest) in promoting that stable relationship with the global ecosystem on which our common survival ultimately depends.

Finally, one must consider the poor. One out of four people in the world lives from day to day without knowing where the next meal is coming from, whether their children will be properly clothed, or whether they will find adequate shelter from one day to the next. Within developing countries, the more affluent classes, and those centered in the cities, tend to dominate the rural poor completely; in general, laws and customs coincide in assuring the continuation of such domination. The outcome of this negligence of the poor is that their ranks are swelling rapidly. What is wrong with such strategies, such attitudes?

First, they are morally indefensible. Faced with the facts, most people would find the death of 40,000 babies each day unacceptable. There is no justification for the bigoted view that these deaths prevent the world from becoming over-populated: The world is already overpopulated, and a study of history indicates clearly that people who lead orderly lives are most able to control their own numbers and will do so in their own self-interest.

Second, for us to allow so many to starve, to go hungry, and to live in absolute poverty, is to threaten the future of the global ecosystem that sustains us all. Although each person who lives in an industrialized country has a far greater impact on the global ecosystem than each person who lives in a developing country, everyone must have a reasonable share of the earth's productivity or our civilization will simply come unraveled.

Some Specific Solutions

Many aspects of the collective action that we must undertake are so obvious that they need little elaboration here. **Population stability** must be attained throughout the world, and the industrialized countries must assist others in carrying out their plans in this respect. It is especially important for industrialized countries to attain stable population levels, since their people consume such a disproportionately large share of what the world is capable of producing. There is no hope for a peaceful world without overall population stability, and no hope for regional ecological sustainability without regional population stability.

As mentioned earlier, *a rising standard of living, coupled with the fuller expression of women's rights everywhere,* would greatly accelerate the attainment of global population stability. We must clearly work toward the abandonment of the mad view that only rapid population growth everywhere will make possible economic progress and prosperity. Prosperity throughout the world must be attained as a result of an enhanced degree of global sharing, substituted at least in part for international competitiveness and greed.

A special word needs to be said about *the control of disease*. The increasingly dense human population affords special opportunities for the rapid spread of diseases, especially viral diseases—difficult to control—on a global scale. This poses unique dangers for the human prospect beyond the year 2000, and constitutes a problem that requires urgent attention from both a scientific and a societal level. It should be pointed out, however, that diseases are unlikely to control worldwide population growth, much less to reverse it. Some ill-informed people actually speak about AIDS, in Africa for example, as if it were some sort of ghastly "solution" to the problems of poverty and starvation that have become endemic there. Even in the most highly affected parts of Africa, however, the highest estimates of the incidence of the AIDS virus are about 5 percent; with an annual population growth of just under 3 percent in tropical Africa generally, it can readily be seen why AIDS will not reverse or "solve" the problems we have been discussing.

Energy use must be rationalized throughout the world. The greenhouse effect associated with increasing concentrations of carbon dioxide and other gases in the atmosphere ought to stimulate research into alternative energy sources. Even if we officially choose to assume that the supply of fossil fuels such as oil and coal is infinite, burning them in the quantities that we now consume is certainly not an environmentally sound practice. Energy production by nuclear fusion, safer methods of utilizing nuclear fission to provide energy, and solar energy, including biomass production—all of these methods should be explored, and a global plan for stable energy use should be developed and implemented cooperatively while there is still a little breathing room.

Our consideration of energy brings us to the point of *international cooperation* overall. The UNEP-sponsored agreement on the protection of the ozone layer, mentioned earlier, constitutes a very significant model for the development of similar agreements in other areas. The Tropical Forest Action Plan is another example of an international scheme to achieve common goals. The report of the World Commission on Environment and Development to the General Assembly of the United Nations (1987) represents a very significant step in the process of considering common problems in an appropriate, governmental, collective context. Such efforts should be encouraged strongly: They indicate the framework of what will be necessary if we are to attain a relatively secure future by the end of the century.

More obvious is the need for the development of *plans for the sustainable use of the soils and water* of all regions of the world, and the provision of adequate schemes for sustainable agriculture and forestry everywhere. The needs for agricultural products cannot be provided by overproduction in industrial, temperate countries, which have erected bizarre financial structures to subsidize their farmers beyond all reason, and which seem unwilling to go very far in assisting those who live in developing countries. These developing countries, however, can achieve stability only if their best lands—those that are capable of sustainable productivity— are developed properly, and if appropriate land-use schemes are worked out and implemented everywhere. Many experts agree that all of the agriculture and forestry needs of the poor

177

people who live in the tropics could certainly be met by a proper development of lands that have already been deforested.

Biotechnology affords remarkable new opportunities for the improvement of agricultural and forestry systems, and should be utilized widely in the development of improved crops throughout the world. We simply cannot afford our current, relatively inefficient use of our resources, nor the hunger that results from insufficient supplies of food in many regions. A global effort should be made to utilize the tools that are available to us now for the improvement of many traditional tropical crops, such as cassava and yams, and for the development of additional ones that can be used in areas not now under cultivation.

Finally, steps must be taken to *prevent massive extinction.* How can we help to reverse the tide?

The creation and maintenance of protected areas throughout the world is obviously one important ingredient in the process. For such areas to persist, however, they must be regarded both by their immediate neighbors, by the people of their countries, and by world opinion as indispensable and worth supporting. In fact, the people of relatively poor countries are often anxious to preserve natural areas, understanding their role in the national patrimony. With widespread poverty, however, the process is difficult. The implementation of agro-forestry schemes and other methods of sustainable productivity around or even within such areas, properly designed, can contribute in an important way to their success. Environmental education is an indispensable component of the acceptance of such areas in all countries and must be pursued fully everywhere. Studies of the characteristics of populations and the other factors involved in preserving and managing specific ecosystems must be accelerated and the results put into practice; for example, the protected areas must be large enough to accommodate viable populations of the species that are being protected.

Ex situ preservation—the preservation of selected samples of species of organisms away from the areas where they occur naturally—could be an important strategy in our overall effort to preserve biological diversity. There are some efforts to preserve a few dozen important crops and their wild relatives in seed banks and other genetic stock centers, for example, but no overall effort to save other plants that might prove even more important in feeding us in the future, or supplying us with other valuable commodities, than those our Stone Age ancestors first domesticated. Selected samples of seeds of plant families that are known for their economic importance, such as legumes (peas), palms, and grasses, for example, ought to be obtained as a matter of global concern, stored, and made freely available to all legitimate users.

INDIVIDUAL VALUES

On reaching the year 2000, humans will be able to view the future somewhat optimistically only if they have taken steps to achieve stable population levels; to develop a global plan for the sustainable use of energy; and to have put in place national and regional agricultural and forestry projects capable of meeting the needs of their people. To do this will require an unprecedented effort, but one that is clearly necessary. In order for such an effort to be made, however, there must first be an adjustment in individual values.

In the 1980s, major concern is being expressed about values—about what they are, how they are changing, and about the ways in which society in general and the educational system in particular imparts them to people. These values are central to our theme, because they underlie the ways in which we are able to cooperate with one another as we respond to the challenges that are so clearly confronting us.

The 1987 Cooperative Institutional Research Program of the American Council on Education revealed some trends than many find disturbing. For example, among freshmen entering universities in the U.S. in 1967, 83 percent considered the development of a meaningful philosophy of life as an essential or very important goal; in 1987, less than 40 percent of entering freshmen shared this view. Correspondingly, in 1987, 76 percent of entering freshmen regarded being very well-off financially as essential or very important to them, a figure that was nearly double the proportion of entering freshmen who shared this view in 1970.

There are, however, intelligent and highly motivated people among the freshmen, as among citizens of all countries. Their leadership activities are more important now than ever. Citizens and their representatives increasingly are called on to make decisions about complex scientific and technological issues. The educational system must prepare them for this role, because we need the very best effort we are capable of. Ignorance bolstered by a general feeling that science is somehow cold and irrelevant will not suffice to make the decisions critical to our survival in the future, regardless of how comfortable it may make us feel.

According to poll after poll, people in the United States are committed to the principle of increased governmental intervention to protect the environment. According to environmental polls conducted by Louis Harris, 92 percent of the people in this country believe that hazardous waste is a serious problem, 86 percent are concerned about contaminated drinking water, and 79 percent consider acid rain and nuclear wastes important problems. A recent poll of West Germans revealed that 85 percent believe that the environment is a close second to unemployment as an important national problem. Worldwide, Green parties and similar environmental groups are gaining credibility and political power; the first international Green Congress, with about two hundred delegates from seventeen countries, was held in Stockholm in August 1987. United by their opposition to nuclear power and their desire to conserve natural resources, Greens serve as a lightning rod for environmentalists of all ages. In addition, nongovernmental organizations throughout the world are gaining power as political forces favoring sustainable development in place of a quick payoff.

Religious and ethical leaders are coming to grips with problems of the environment, motivated in part by their shared desire for social justice and by the realization that we may, after all, be only one element in the global ecosystem rather than some sort of mysteriously self-sustaining entity not subject to biological laws. In the words of Robin Wright, in *The Christian Science Monitor* for November 4, 1987: "The continuum of various faiths, which have survived centuries and outlived hundreds of political dynasties, provides ideals by which to determine goals." In his splendid book on the ways in which we are responding and should respond to the cultural and economic forces that dominate our society, Daniel Yankelovich has written, most appropriately, that "we need new rules to encourage people to channel their creativity away from themselves and back onto the concrete tasks that need doing in the new era."

In taking up this task, we are all inspired by idealistic individuals (or are they realists?) such as the tree-huggers of the Chipko movement in northern India, who well realize the value of forests — symbolic of a sustainable environment — and are taking personal action to try to save them. In short, there is worldwide enthusiasm about conserving the environment, but the means for focusing this enthusiasm and funding it at the global level that it requires remain problems for the future.

In confronting the massive problems that have been discussed in this paper, we are led inexorably to the necessity for international cooperation—a shared realization of our common humanity—so that we can properly manage the earth for our common benefit. A world in which the annual military budget of all countries combined equals the income of 2.6 billion people in the forty-four poorest nations, or one in which 2,900 times as much money is spent on national military forces as on international peace-keeping efforts, is a world in which it is very difficult to chart the outlines of future survival. Despite the extreme military threat, however, we must work out the ecological principles on which human survival depends and put them into action globally. The need to do so is ultimately an individual human responsibility: Every person has a role to play in the assault that our times require.

I appreciate the advice of Donald Kennedy, C. Peter Magrath, Tamra Engelhorn Raven, and Bassam Shakhashiri in the course of preparation of this paper.

Bibliography

Brandt, W. *Arms and Hunger.* New York: Pantheon Books, 1986.

Brown, L. R. et al. *State of the World, 1988.* New York: W. W. Norton & Company, 1988.

Grant, J. P. *The State of the World's Children, 1988.* New York: UNICEF, Division of Information and Public Affairs, 1988.

Kidder, R. M. *An Agenda for the 21st Century.* Cambridge, Mass.: MIT Press, 1987.

Leopold, A. *A Sand County Almanac.* New York: Oxford University Press, 1966.

Population *1987 World Population Data Sheet.* Washington, D.C.: 1987 Reference Bureau, Inc.

Repetto, R. "Creating Incentives for Sustainable Forest Development." *Ambio* 16 (1987): pp. 94–99.

Soule, M., Gilpin, M., Conway, W., and Foose, T. "The Millennium Ark: How Long A Voyage, How Many Staterooms, How Many Passengers?" *Zoo Biology* 5 (1986): pp. 101–113.

Vitousek, P. M., Ehrlich, P. R., Ehrlich, A. H., and Matson, P. A. "Human Appropriation of the Products of Photosynthesis." *BioScience* 36 (1986): 368–373.

Wilson, E. O. (ed.) *Biodiversity.* Washington, D.C.: National Academy Press, 1988.

World Commission on Environment and Development. *Our Common Future.* New York: Oxford University Press, 1987.

Endnotes

Chapter 1

1. Lapidus's paper, along with the two other conference papers by Rodrigo Botero and Peter Raven, appears in the Appendices.

2. *North-South: A Programme for Survival* (London: Pan Books, 1980), p. 19.

3. *Our Common Future* (New York: Oxford University Press, 1987), p. 4.

4. *Ibid.,* p. 22.

Appendix 1

1. *Partners in Development: Report of the Commission on International Development* (New York: Praeger, 1969).

2. David Morawetz, *Twenty-five Years of Economic Development; 1950–1975* (Washington, D.C.: World Bank Books, 1977).

3. *Ibid.*

4. *North-South: A Programme for Survival* (London: Pan Books, 1980).

Appendix 2

1. For a more extensive treatment, see the author's "State and Society: Toward the Emergence of Civil Society in the Soviet Union," in *Politics, Society and Nationality Inside Gorbachev's Russia* (Westview, 1989). For a similar argument concerning China, see Richard Baum, "Modernization and Legal Reform in Post-Mao China: The Rebirth of Socialist Legality," *Studies in Comparative Communism,* 19:2 (Summer 1986).

2. K. U. Chernenko, *Kommunist* (13 September 1981), pp. 10–11; Mikhail Gorbachev, *Pravda,* January 31, 1987.

3. Tsentral'noe statisticheskoe unpravlenie, Narodnoe khoziastvo-USSSR v 1985Q. (Moscow: *Statistika,* 1985), pp. 27–28, 64.

4. The Party Program adopted in 1961 was the quintessential expression of Khrushchev's unbounded optimism, with its extravagant prediction that in twenty years Soviet economic output would outstrip that of the United States, and its promise that the Soviet population would enjoy material abundance. The most striking feature of the new Party programs adopted under Gorbachev is the modesty and lack of concreteness of its goals.

5. *Pravda,* February 6, 1987.

6. Aleksandr Vasinsky, in *Izvestia,* October 18, 1986.

7. Speech to the Trade Union Congress, *Pravda,* February 26, 1987.

8. Vladivostok speech, *Pravda,* July 29, 1986.

9. *Pravda,* January 28, 1987.

10. *Pravda,* February 26, 1987.

Index

Poverty, 19–20, 29, 31, 88, 93
    goals for, 100, 103
Privatization of economy, in
    Soviet Union, 94
Protein engineering. *See*
    Genetic technology.

Quality of life, 32, 81, 97

Racism, 95
Radcliffe College, 9
Raven, Peter, 19, 60–61
Reagan, Ronald, 64
"Rent" for environmental
    resources. *See* Conserva-
    tion easements.
Republican Party, 77
Resource allocation. *See* Global
    resources, allocation of.
Resource management, 96
Robert Kennedy Human Rights
    Award, 11
Rosenberg, Tina, 10, 108, 109
Royal Society of Medicine
    (London), 85
Rule of law, in developing
    nations, 83
Rural populations, 48, 56, 59,
    81, 94

Saudi Arabia, 27–28
School dropouts, 93
Sea level, and global warming
    trend, 55
Security. *See* Global security.
Shippey, Kim, 10
Short-term thinking, 47, 110
Sitcoms, on USSR, 96
Social Democratic Party (Great
    Britain), 11
Social and Liberal Democrats
    (Great Britain), 11

Social Security, 77–78, 97
Social services, in developing
    nations, 20
Solar energy, 51, 56, 58
Solid waste, 57
Sophia University (Tokyo), 9
Sophocles, 5
South Korea, 31
Southern Women's Rural
    Network, 11
Species conservation, 52,
    104–105
Sri Lanka, 20, 25
Stalin, Joseph, 2, 34
Stanford University, 8, 10, 87
Starvation, 30, 78
Stevens, Wallace, 8
Stravinsky, Igor, 84
Successor generation, 12
Superpowers
    behavior of, 94
    concept of, 42
    cooperation between, 103
    ethics in, 73
    relations between, 93, 95
    responsibilities of, 46

Tanzania, 25
Technology
    appropriate, 57–59, 70
    education about, 58–59, 96
    in developing nations, 41, 83
    large-scale, 58
Terrorism, 103
Thailand, 18
Third World. *See* Developing
    nations.
Tobacco use, 64
Townsend, Kathleen Kennedy,
    11, 82
    on ethics, 74–75
Toxic waste, 52, 67, 105